Connection to the Cosmos:

Remembering Your Galactic Heritage and Embracing Your Oneness

by Dr. Lisa Thompson

As You Wish Publishing
Phoenix, AZ
Cover photography and digital art: Ashton Miyako
Cover design by: As You Wish Publishing
Interior design by: As You Wish Publishing
Author portrait by: Ashton Miyako
Drawing of Arcturian Uluru with Lisa: Tiffany Guinn
ISBN: 978-1-951131-50-0
Library of Congress Control Number: 2022913231
www.DrLisaJThompson.com

CONTENTS

FOREWORD
by Sunny Dawn Johnston

I was honored to be asked by Lisa to write this foreword – for several reasons. I have known Lisa for several years and I have witnessed her growth and expansion. When we met, she was a successful businesswoman, and deepening her connection to Spirit - and all that it encompasses - with passion and drive. In a matter of just a couple of years, she went from a client and student of mine to a colleague and expert in her field. Her field has also expanded and grown as she has remembered and embraced her "non-traditional" journey. Lisa, as you will read in this book, was born into an unconventional family environment that offered her a different perspective on life, one that many people could not understand … at least at that time. The beauty is that not only did she acknowledge it, but she also used her experience and knowledge to support and help others with their own experiences and mis-understanding of the cosmos and their connection to other non-earth realms.

Throughout my career as a psychic medium, I have come across hundreds of people that had "extraterrestrial" experiences but were scared to share them … even with me. They would whisper about them in our private appointments or share them only in a space where they felt completely safe for fear of judgment, ridicule, or downright harassment. They knew what they knew and what they felt, but they didn't know what it all meant. I understood how they felt, as I too had galactic experiences that I didn't understand, but knew were real and true.

Lisa's newest book, *Connection to the Cosmos*, helps you to recognize that the feelings you may have had - when younger, or even more recently - were because you are connected cosmically. You may not yet understand the signs you are receiving; maybe you haven't known what to call it, but you know that we are not alone on this planet Earth. You know there is something greater out there.

Through Lisa's personal experience and in-depth study, she will help you understand how to work with galactic energy. Just reading this book, I believe, will activate that part of you that feels connected. It will help you to let go of who or what you thought you were ... to open up to who you truly are and where you came from. When you understand your connection to the cosmos you will then be able to release the fear and open up to be of greater service to all, both on earth and in the vastness of the universe.

What is really great about this book is that it breaks down the cosmos into four major areas of exploration. Lisa gives you just enough information for the newcomer to understand some of the basics and not feel overwhelmed. At the same time, there is plenty of new information for those that are already seasoned in the language and understanding of the Galactic world.

The information is easily digestible in these four areas. The first is personal stories and experiences with the cosmos that I believe help you identify and possibly see yourself through her experiences. She even shares how she was able to embrace and integrate it all into this current life journey.

The second area creates a foundation for the terminology that is used, as well as the basic concepts. This helps you understand the UFO and alien phenomena from a higher perspective. I think that this area is key for many people, as society has trained us to be fearful. Most people are fearful of what they don't understand. With Lisa's help and her sharing of this information, it creates a safe environment to learn and let go of the fear. In the third area, Lisa introduces you to some of our galactic family and friends. She also includes a great summary of the evolution of the human, which is fascinating. And lastly, Lisa gives you specific tools and practices to further grow in your connection to your alien guides and includes tips on how to open up to receive their guidance as well.

Lisa has done a beautiful job of bringing together the data, the experience, the connection, and the wisdom and has distilled it down for you to take in. If you have felt the calling ... if you have had unusual experiences you can't explain ... if you have always been fascinated by the night sky or the UFO talk – this book will help you put the pieces of the puzzle together and bring you to greater insights than you ever thought possible.

The courage Lisa has shown to bring these experiences and information forward and to be of greater service to humanity is truly a gift to us all. For, as we know, we are ALL one!!! Now it's time to dive in ... and see what you discover within yourself.

~ Sunny Dawn Johnston – Psychic Medium, Spiritual Mentor and Author of *Invoking the Archangels* **and** *The Love Never Ends*

INTRODUCTION
Connecting to the Cosmos

"It has been said that once the mind has been expanded by an idea or concept, it can never return to its original way of thinking." — Dolores Cannon, Five Lives Remembered

Have you ever looked up in the sky and questioned if there is other life out there beyond our Earth? Do you look at the sky and yearn for something more? Do you ever feel like your home is somewhere else beyond Earth? Have you been told that you're a *Starseed*? Do you feel like you are connected cosmically but want to understand the signs you are receiving?

I always had an innate knowing we were not alone in the Universe. I felt like I was from beyond this Earth, but I didn't know why or how. What I know now is we are not alone. There is so much more to reality than our Earthly third-dimensional experiences.

I am honored to be able to share my knowledge and experiences with you. I am here on Earth as an *Arcturian Starseed*, with many parallel lives in other non-Earth realms. If you are confused about what that means, you will learn all of this and more.

I have been an "experiencer" my entire life. What is an experiencer? It is one who has had a direct connection with one or more alien/extraterrestrial races. I grew up in a spiritual school of enlightenment, which completely opened my world to experiencing other realities beyond Earth. My first conscious interaction with a different alien race was when I was 15 years old and was taken in a craft. I met my Arcturian family almost four years ago. In addition to having contact, I have witnessed numerous spacecraft throughout my life in different locations and instances around the world.

Last year I had a DNA activation which now allows me to speak *Light Language* through my hands and is slowly coming through my voice. I also recently began vocally channeling an Arcturian collective. I have experienced living parallel lives in other parts of the universe and connections with multiple groups of beings inside and beyond Earth.

Coming Out of the Proverbial Closet

I have always been fascinated with the night sky and the potential for life on other planets and star systems. I was also obsessed with the diversity of life on our own planet, particularly the animals. I learned as much as I could about animals as a child, and the more strange or unusual the animal was, the more I loved it.

My passion for animals on Earth drove me to my first career in zoology/marine biology. I received my PhD from the University of Chicago and the Field Museum of Natural History. The more I learned about the untapped biodiversity on our planet, even with millions of known species identified, particularly in the oceans and the rain forests, the more I knew for certain there had to be life beyond our Earth.

INTRODUCTION

The academic and natural history museum world I was immersed in was focused on discovering the unknown species out there. My professors and cohorts were constantly discovering new species. We were also looking at the evolution of these animals and how they operated at a biomechanical and physiological level.

Even with some of the incredible research being done at the time, the mindset in our university and museum departments was very limited. They believed we could discover more of the already "known" groups of typical animals, but anything outside of the norm was considered taboo. This includes sasquatch (bigfoot), yeti, mermaids, and others of the cryptozoology world.

I was fairly vocal about my belief in the potential existence of these creatures, but my fellow scientists were not on the same page. When I shared my personal experiences with UFOs, aliens, ghosts and other paranormal activities with my science friends, they thought I was crazy. I did not fit into mainstream academia, and I did not fit in with this group of people.

In my home state of Washington, I knew several people who had had experiences with sasquatch, and I completely believed them and their accounts of what happened. I also had a few friends in college that had experienced a lot of different paranormal activity in their homes and elsewhere. I knew their experiences were real, as were mine. Even if science didn't have a way to prove the existence of something, it couldn't take away our real experiences.

There was also the question in anthropology about the "missing link" to our modern-day humans. Where was it?

What was it? I spent six years at the Field Museum of Natural History, where they had a display of the evolution of humanoids with the famous "Lucy" on display, but no missing link. Although I wasn't in this specific field of science, it was a curiosity for me.

Looking back now, I can see how all of the education I received in biology allowed me to understand how animals had developed and adapted to their environments. I knew there was so much more to discover that our science did not have the capability of tapping into. It helped me to solidify my appreciation for life on Earth, as well as on other planets and worlds.

It took nearly 50 years for me to feel comfortable sharing my connection with the cosmos. After leaving academia, my careers were in the mainstream fields of mortgage and interior design. I didn't share my stories because I wanted to be taken seriously. The majority of my life had been wrapped up in presenting myself to the world in the way in which I thought I would be accepted by my peer groups, which meant hiding parts of me that did not fit the group dynamic.

A year and a half ago, I moved to Hawaii from Washington state. With this move, I feel like I have been able to come out of the proverbial closet, so to speak. I knew when I arrived on the island, it was time to step into my full authentic, weird, wild self, no matter what anyone else was going to think.

The final release of my old paradigm of disguising myself occurred when I liquidated my design company, Design Smart, in 2021. This was the final thread to my former life, holding me back from showing up fully in my light, experience, and wisdom. Once the weight was lifted, the final mask was tossed aside.

Now it's time for me to show the world who and what I truly am without apology, without exception, and without any worry that I will not fit in. My purpose is much larger than I could have ever imagined it to be growing up, and I am ready to live that purpose.

I am a Galactic Ambassador helping you to find your place in the cosmos. I am here to help change the fear-based narrative the government and media are presenting in their "disclosure." I am here to share the message that love is the root of all existence, and we are all one. There is no separation. It is only a figment of our 3D-based reality. Our galactic family is here to support us. They are not here to harm us.

In my role as a Galactic Ambassador, I teach in a variety of formats. My husband and I lead UFO tours in our Hawaii-based business, Big Island UFO Tours. Under my umbrella of Mystic Manta, LLC, I am an intuitive transformational coach specializing in past life regression therapy and human design. I teach online classes, lead retreats, write blogs and books, and guide people through regressions to recover their hidden memories of parallel lives and contact experiences. I help people connect with their own galactic family and guides and to upgrade and activate their latent DNA. I share my story so those reading it or hearing it don't feel like they are crazy in their own experiences. I want to normalize this reality.

The information I present in this book is to help you open your mind and consciousness to expand your reality. I share general information about what extraterrestrials and extradimensionals are and why they are interacting with us. I include my personal stories, as they may help you to understand your own experiences. I also provide you with tools and techniques which can help you in your Earth-based life, as well as in deepening your interaction with your galactic family. I am here as a facilitator to help you remember who and what you are and activate you to a higher vibration of living.

Misconception Versus Truth

There is a lot of information, both good and bad, out there about extraterrestrials, aliens, UFOs and similar phenomena. Everything I teach comes from a combination of personal experiences, journeys, teachings from Ascended Masters and galactic entities via channeling, and research. Other people may have very different ideas and experiences, so take what resonates with you.

With all that I have experienced and the wisdom I have gained, I know LOVE is the true nature of our universe. When you are watching something on TV or the internet, reading, or listening to information regarding UFOs and extraterrestrials, I invite you to examine it from a higher perspective to understand if the message is coming from a place of love or from fear. Really pay attention to the words and phrases used (i.e., scary, fear, attack, eerie, etc.). Use your inner knowingness to discern the information.

INTRODUCTION

The fear-based messaging around this topic in the media, Hollywood, and government is to control your thinking. It is to keep those in power feeling like they have the power. Ultimately, you have total control and power over your life. How your frequency vibrates determines what situations and experiences are coming into your life. If you live in fear, you attract fear. When you come from a place of love, you experience love all around you.

Ultimately, we are all one. We come from Source. Imagine, if you will, the universe as a giant disco ball with all the tiny mirrors that make it sparkle. Each of you is looking out of one of those tiny windows. Those residing close together share a similar perspective. Those residing on the opposite side see something very different. Everyone is part of this disco ball. Everyone and everything are connected. We are just tiny fragments of the whole, having our own personal experiences to feed back into the one Source. I am everyone, but I'm having an individual experience. You are everyone having an individual experience.

What to Expect From This Book

There are huge benefits to understanding and working with galactic energy. We are here to be human, but we are also here to wake up and remember who we truly are and where we came from. Understanding our connection to the cosmos helps to overcome the fear of the possible existence of extraterrestrials and their interactions with Earth.

I have broken the book down into four major sections. In Section 1, I share personal stories and experiences of embracing who I am and integrating it into this Earth life.

Section 2 provides a foundation of terminology and concepts to help you understand the UFO and alien phenomena from a higher perspective. Section 3 is an introduction to some of our galactic family and friends. It also includes a meditative journey to meet your galactic family and guides. Section 4 gives you specific tools and practices to enhance your ability to connect to and receive guidance from your alien guides. It also includes a journey to activate your DNA for stronger connection, as well as a journey to experience your parallel non-Earth lives.

The truth is out there, and even more importantly, the truth is inside of us. It's time to remember your galactic heritage and embrace your oneness.

SECTION 1: REMEMBERING AND EMBRACING WHO I AM

Chapter 1
Ramtha—A Channeled Ascended
Master from Lemuria

*"But I am here to help you realize that you are indeed an
ongoing, immortal essence who has been living billions of
years ever since God, your beloved Father, the totality of
thought, contemplated itself into the brilliance of light,
which each of you became."*
— Ramtha, Ramtha—The White Book

I grew up in a household that was not anything like the
homes my friends were in. My parents divorced when I
was two, and my mom moved me from Colorado to
Oklahoma City to be near her sister. My mom grew up in
the Southern Baptist church but left the church when she
married my dad. Soon after we arrived in Oklahoma, she
started a new journey of learning astrology. She took
regular classes and was part of the study groups she would
take me to. Her friends were active metaphysical
practitioners of astrology, numerology, tarot, and witch-
craft. I spent hours with her in the local metaphysical store,
Starwind, in those early years.

It was in 1985 when my mom was first introduced to
Ramtha via video and audio tape recordings. Ramtha is a
channeled entity who speaks through a woman named JZ
Knight. Ramtha claims he lived an Earth life about 35,000
years ago as a male warrior from Lemuria during the time

of Atlantis. His army was at war with Atlantis, and he has said that those who are now attracted to his energy and teachings had once been members of his army. After a severe injury, he spent several years healing and observing the ways of the Universe and became an Ascended Master.

Ramtha, as a channeled entity, gained notoriety in the 1980s when JZ Knight went into a trance state and channeled Ramtha on national television on the Merv Griffin show. Actresses Shirley MacLaine, Linda Evans, and Salma Hayek have been part of the student body. MacLaine talks about her relationship with Ramtha in her books, *Out on a Limb* and *Dancing in the Light.* At the height of the Ramtha School's popularity, there were more than 10,000 followers from around the world.

The same year my mom and aunt went to an in-person weekend Ramtha event being held in Colorado called "The Days to Come." In that channeled seminar, they were given information that would completely change the trajectory of our lives. The general message was at some point in the near future, things would be bad on the Earth, and those who wanted to survive would need to be able to live off the land and have access to a lot of fresh water.

When they came home from the weekend, they had already decided we needed to move away from Oklahoma. After considering different places, they ended up choosing to move to Washington state to be near Ramtha. Another benefit of Washington is it has plenty of rainfall.

We moved to Yelm, Washington, in the summer of 1986 when I was 13 and just starting eighth grade. At the time, I was angry about the move. I had been named head cheerleader at my school, and I didn't want to leave my friends. Although I had initial resistance to seeing what Ramtha was about—due in part to thinking my mother was a little crazy—my curiosity overcame my anger for the move to a new state, and I attended my first event.

This event was a personal question-and-answer session where there were only 100 people in attendance, held at JZ's house around her indoor swimming pool. We were able to ask a specific question to Ramtha if we chose to. Although I had never experienced anything like this, I could feel the energy coming out of JZ's body. It was definitely a stronger, more powerful energy than any human I had ever met. I knew right then this was not just acting. There was a real energy being channeled.

As Ramtha walked around the room, he came closer to where my mother and I sat. He looked directly at me. I felt paralyzed and couldn't speak. It was as if he was looking into the depths of my soul and saw me for who I really was beyond the physical body. He read my mind and answered my question without me needing to ask it out loud. I wasn't sure what to think, but I was intrigued.

After my first Ramtha session, I had the opportunity to attend many more events. We learned about the nature of reality and how manifestation works. We learned we are the creators of our reality. We are all God—God is within. There is no separation. We are mirrors and teachers for each other. We also learned about other dimensions of time and space. We learned about other living and energy beings, including extraterrestrials, fairies, and other dimensional entities. These were some of my favorite teachings.

The first discipline we learned in the school was a process called C&E. It represents that consciousness plus energy creates the nature of reality, so it is a manifestation practice. We would do this process for hours on end during the events. The idea was to raise our energy up through our spine, moving through our chakras (Ramtha refers to them as seals, not chakras), and out through the top of our heads. Although I was physically fit as a teenager, my body did not enjoy doing this discipline for the long hours we spent. Mantras, affirmations, and visualizations were also part of this discipline.

At the age of 16, I decided I had learned enough information from Ramtha at the time, and I wanted to just be a normal teenager. It didn't sink in until I was a young adult how powerful the information was that I had learned, and it would create a foundation and pathway to under-standing the universe in a much larger capacity than what the mainstream world knew about.

After leaving the Ramtha teachings when I was 16, I was reintroduced at the age of 28. I had just finished my PhD in biology, and I was a post-doctoral researcher at the Field Museum in Chicago. I planned a trip back to Washington state to visit my mom for Christmas that year.

For my birthday present, my mom scheduled an appointment with her chiropractor in Yelm. He contacted me a week or so before my visit to ask me out on a date while I was in town, as he had heard all about me from my mother and had seen my picture. I said yes.

The chiropractor was a very active part of the Ramtha School, and knowing my science background, he shared with me the new information being taught in the school. It was all about brain physiology, epigenetics, and quantum mechanics. This piqued my interest, and I decided to learn more.

This started a five-year journey in the Ramtha School as an adult, soaking up as much information as I could. The School had changed quite a bit since my teenage years in terms of the information being taught. As a teenager, it was more ethereal, spiritual concepts. As an adult, it was a lot of the science underlying the spiritual concepts, which I, with my science background, very much appreciated.

After my post-doc in Chicago was over, I moved to Springfield, Ohio, where I had a tenure-track professor position. I was flying to Washington when I could to attend events, and ultimately I decided I needed to move back to Washington to immerse myself fully into the teachings.

There were more disciplines and practices we learned in the new era of the School, in addition to the original C&E work. Some of the practices we were doing included remote viewing, telepathy and mind-reading, candle work, mirror work (very different from what Louise Hay teaches), fieldwork, blind-folded archery, and grid work, among other things.

We learned how to interact with and call in entities from other dimensions and how to communicate with them. There were thousands of photos taken during the events showing orbs, plasma, and entities in the audience with us. We did exercises where we would draw a symbol on a card (everyone had their own symbol), and the orbs would respond by creating those symbols inside the orb bubble. It was incredible!

In doing the grid work, I was able to see through the veil to other dimensions where I could witness spacecraft in front of me. I was regularly leaving my body in astral projection. I was able to go inward to experience the void and understand who and what we truly are.

Outside of the School, I often had my own interactions with these entities. I would call them in and then take photos. This was a common thing in my life at that time. The work we were doing was also opening up my mind to having other kinds of visions, including other lives I had/was living.

Although I had learned so much from the school, at the age of 33, it was time for me to leave once again and go out live the teachings. I have not returned to the Ramtha teachings since that time, but I have been able to integrate the information I learned into my life to a certain degree. There was always a lot of controversy around Ramtha and JZ Knight. While I knew what we were learning about the universe and our origins was truth (you know how you have a deep knowing of truth when you hear or experience something), there was also a lot of fear being taught I didn't buy into. Some of the fear-based messaging continues to this day.

My opinion and experience of Ramtha are that most of the messages are truth and love-based, reflecting the nature of the Universe and how it came to be and who we really are. Although I was indoctrinated, not all of the messages were bad. I appreciate that I have the ability to take what works and what is true for me and leave the rest behind. I use this in all things I learn about. This is what I help teach people to do for themselves. We all have the answers inside. We just need to know how to listen and trust those answers when they come. It's a continual practice.

Since "growing up" with Ramtha, I have had the pleasure of getting to know other channels and really understand what channeling is. We all channel to a certain extent. Some do it through art, music, or other creative endeavors, some through writing, and some through verbally communicating.

When I am listening to or reading channeled information, I get really clear on whether the message is one of love and unity or if it is based in fear. I purposely choose to stay away from the lower vibration of those who channel duality and fear.

I resonate with the messages of my Arcturian guides and other higher dimensional galactic entities. When I see things from the higher perspective, it is easier to view the polarization of the third dimensional Earth in a neutral light and understand that all souls incarnated have a choice when they come here. They sign up for what they experience. It is not for us to judge why. I am here to shine my light. The challenging experiences growing up and in adulthood were so I could work through those situations to be a wayshower for those still in the dark, with full love and compassion.

Chapter 2
Meeting My First Alien Race

"Look at the sky. We are not alone. The whole universe is friendly to us and conspires only to give the best to those who dream and work."
— A. P. J. Abdul Kalam

When I was 15, I had my first conscious experience of meeting a different alien race. On this unforgettable journey, I was taken in a small, shuttle-style spacecraft with one pilot. He appeared to me as a young adult human (perhaps age 20) with dark hair. The ship walls were transparent, so as we were flying through space, it looked like we were flying in a clear bubble. I could clearly see the blackness of space and the beautiful colors of the different gas layers as we headed to our destination, Io, one of Jupiter's moons. I was in awe of the beauty, and I felt completely safe and at ease on this ship with my guide.

Io, which is one of the four largest moons of Jupiter, is actually extremely volatile, with the largest volcanic activity in our solar system. It's an unlikely place to have life, so those who live there must live inside of the moon. That's where we went—inside.

Once we arrived in the interior, I was shown around what looked like a hospital or clinic type of place. There were a few other Earth humans I could see on hospital beds in individual rooms wearing gowns. The hospital staff all appeared as humans. On this trip, I was simply taken on a tour of the hospital rather than being examined myself.

I asked my guide why we all had been brought there. He told me (telepathically) that we were the chosen ones and were being tested to see if we could tolerate living there with them if something ever happened to the Earth. It was the late 1980s when this experience happened, and there was a lot of volatility on the Earth at that time, with World War III pending with nuclear weapons. I found out later, through a mediumship session with my friend, Lee Michael, that those of us who were chosen had a frequency closely matching theirs.

I questioned my guide about their race—were they human or something else? He told me they were humanoid, but not human. They were able to camouflage themselves as humans so as not to scare those who were visitors there, including me. He didn't specifically tell me where they were from, and I didn't think to ask at that time.

I asked him to show me what they really looked like, as I was highly curious and not afraid. When he transformed into his true form, he was about seven feet tall with pure white skin, dark eyes, and very red hair. He had triad-shaped tattoos on his cheeks. On the underside of the tongue was a thorn-shaped fleshy piece. He was wearing a silvery-white uniform with a geometric shape on the front chest. I wasn't scared at all, just intrigued. I felt a strong connection to him like I knew him somehow.

At the end of the journey, the ship returned me home, and I vaguely remember the craft in my backyard. At the time, we lived on 20 acres in the woods in Yelm, Washington. I remember waking up in my bed thinking what a really weird dream I had had. For several months, I continued to think it was just a dream, so I didn't tell anyone about it. Then, I read the book *Communion* by Whitley Strieber. In his book, he talked about his abduction experiences by the gray aliens. At the end of the book, he has a section where he interviews different abductees. There was one person interviewed who had a different story from the others that Whitley seemed to be making fun of. The man shared his story of being taken to a moon of Jupiter, being told he was one of the chosen ones. Whitley made a side comment right after, saying, *"I hope it isn't Io."* My guess is it was in reference to how volatile the surface of the moon is.

As I read the sentence in his book, I had chills up and down my body, which was an indication to me of the truth in my experience. I started crying, knowing my dream was actually real. I went to my mom's room and told her about it, knowing she would believe me. She offered to have me talk to someone she knew who attended our spiritual school, the Ramtha School of Enlightenment.

The man she introduced me to had formerly worked for the military or government with extremely high ranking. He was one of the people who knew about the different alien races the government works with. He had left his job at some point to be a part of the Ramtha teachings. There were several others in the school who had left their government and CIA positions to be a part of the school— some started off by infiltrating the school as spies since the school was thought to be a cult.

I recapped my story about what had happened. When I was finished, he told me I had definitely had a real experience. He also shared he was not aware of my particular group of aliens at the time, and there were many more out there not identified yet by our government. My very real experience and my conversation with the government's alien expert solidified my inner knowing we are not alone in the universe, let alone in our own solar system.

Recently, I had the opportunity to get more clarity around this experience in a conversation with my psychic/medium friend, Lee Michael Walczak. We both knew my session with him was going to be completely different than his other clients.

In our session together, he was able to bring in the energy of my guide from Io, so I could ask some questions. It was in this meeting that I came to realize my experience at age 15 was only one of many forgotten experiences. I had been visited throughout my childhood. This explained why I felt connected to them during my conscious journey.

My guide from Io let us know the reason they are not identified by our government is that they do not directly work with the government, and they actually have very little interaction with humans on Earth.

They are not identified by authors who have classified and illustrated different alien races, including Elena Danaan in her book, *A Gift From the Stars: Extraterrestrial Contacts and Guide of Alien Races* and Craig Campobasso in his book, *The Extraterrestrial Species Almanac,* for similar reasons. They are not directly involved with the Galactic

Federation, which Elena Danaan has extensive experience with.

My Io guide did mention they sometimes work with the Arcturians, which makes sense when put into context with my experiences that I will share in the next chapter about the Arcturians. He shared that those of us who had been chosen by them were selected because our DNA was similar to their race and our frequency was similar enough to be compatible. I asked if they were doing hybridization work, and the response he gave was they only do a little bit, but not to any extent like the Zetas are doing.

In the summer of 2021, I had more information come through me in a channeled state about this experience. The white skin of their form was an adaptation to living inside of the moon. The dark eyes were that way due to enlarged pupils to allow more light in to see better underground. Although they did not share what their origin planet or star was, the red hair could have been from the Lyran or Pleiadian lineage. More will be covered about this in a later chapter.

Other authors and channelers have shared information about other galactic and extradimensional beings living inside of a planet or moon, including Venus and Mars, and we have Inner Earth beings here on our own planet. Some of these beings reside in a higher dimension, which is why they can't be detected with our third-dimensional scientific equipment.

There are still so many questions I have about this experience and this race which one day I hope to answer through my own meditations and channeling, as well as working mediums and channelers like my friend Lee. What I do understand is that I was allowed to remember the interaction from when I was 15, so it would plant a seed for the future. It was something I could not forget or deny happening. No matter what anyone else thinks of the experience, I know it was real. It was beautiful. It opened the door for me to explore other dimensions and realities with a more conscious awareness.

Chapter 3
Meeting My Galactic Family
- the Arcturians

"She's a galaxy of bright hues,

and her heart contains

a universe of love.

She is starlight."

— Melody Lee, Moon Gypsy

In early October of 2018, I connected with a different group of galactic entities. I was taking a psychic intuition class from my friend, psychic/medium Lisa Holm. On the first night of class, she led us through a meditative journey to meet the spirit guide, who would be our psychic connection for tapping into universal information.

During this journey, I traveled to a completely different realm where I met a group of beings. There were several of them standing in front of me, with one main entity in front of the group, as the representative of the collective. They had the most beautiful blue skin, with enlarged bald heads, high cheekbones, large eyes, and tall thin bodies. The energy coming from them was pure love.

The sky was a shimmering iridescent dark blue with a blue moon reflecting into the water next to the beach we were standing on. To my left, on the edge of the water, was an incredible crystalline pyramid structure with similar smaller structures on either side – a crystalline pyramid palace.

On this journey, we were to ask for a gift. I was handed a quartz crystal. We were to ask for a message they would like to share. The entity telepathically communicated that I was one of them. They were one of me. There is no separation. We are family.

We were to ask for a name from this psychic guide, and the name I was given was Uluru. At first, I questioned the name, as it was something familiar to me. I have learned not to question, as it is common to be given a name that resonates with us. Uluru happens to be the native Aboriginal name for the giant red rock in the middle of Australia, renamed Ayers Rock later on.

At the time of class, I didn't know all of the different alien races, as I was only really aware of the alien race from Io I had met and the Zetas (grays) made popular in Hollywood and literature. When I came out of the meditation, all I could do was describe in detail what I had seen and experienced. Based on the message I received from Uluru, Lisa suggested I had just met my galactic family. This rang true for me as soon as she said it.

There was a student in my class who was very familiar with different aliens, and she told me that based on my description of the skin color, the group I met was either the Arcturians or the Blue Avians. When I got home after class, I did an internet search. As soon as I saw images of the Arcturians, I knew it was them. It was exactly how they appeared in my vision.

CHAPTER 3 | MEETING MY GALACTIC FAMILY
– THE ARCTURIANS

After meeting my Arcturian family, I had several encounters which helped to validate my experience. Seven months after my experience, I met a highly psychic woman at a retreat I was attending in Bali. She immediately observed me as being galactic when I crossed her path, as she was also galactic. She told me I was a Starseed. A couple of days later, in the retreat, she had a dream about me, but I did not look like this human Lisa. I appeared as a blue being with bright red hair, which reminded me of a cross between Uluru (my Arcturian) and my guide from Io.

There were others who immediately identified me as Arcturian without me saying a word to them. One psychic in Oregon told me directly I was an Arcturian Starseed. My response was, "I know."

I was also at a retreat in Sedona, where I was able to meet a fellow Arcturian Starseed. Matt Kahn, who was one of the retreat speakers, had crossed her path at the retreat and told her very directly she was Arcturian. She didn't know what it meant at the time, and she shared with me what he said. I was able to help her understand a little bit of what it meant. She and I were magnetically drawn to each other (the very first night) at an event of 300 attendees, and we remain in contact to this day.

Right after I moved to Hawaii, I met one of my Arcturian sisters, which was verified in a Regression session with her. I was able to help her identify one of our Arcturian brothers on the island as well. In the last few months of writing this, three independent psychics have shared with me that the Arcturian collective is with me and always there to support me.

In addition to the experiences I share above, I have also gained more insight from sessions with two different healers/channelers. Lee Michael Walczak is a psychic/medium who has become a good friend. In our several sessions together, he has helped me access my Arcturian collective, as well as other galactic beings. Tracie Mahan is a QHHT (Quantum Healing Hypnosis Therapist) practitioner and channels Arcturian Daniel. She has helped me channel information from my higher self and from Uluru regarding many aspects of my parallel lives, discussed here and in the next chapter.

In the original session I did with Lee Michael, who helped me answer questions about my experience on Io, we were able to speak with the Arcturian collective as well, which was elaborated on in a second session.

Channeled message to me and my role from the Arcturians via Lee Michael:

"You are needed right now because your world is at a pivotal, transitional point in history. Your soul came to be in this time and place to be a part of this. Your work is important and appreciated. You must be more within your own energy and show fearlessness like you never have before.

What is happening (on Earth) is causing a rippling effect across the universe. You are here to remind people of their own ability to create in the world and to share the idea that there is interconnected unity. What affects one affects the whole. You are an interconnected web of consciousness. You (as humans) are, in a lot of ways creating what you are seeing. You've lost sight that you are creator beings, and you need to remember your own power around this. You are powerful in your own energy, and that creates the experience of how you experience reality."

Channeled message (through me) regarding my connection to Arcturus during Ascension session with Tracie:

"There is water there, like blue moon or blue sun, something that makes it look iridescent blue there. What is it like to be Arcturian? Pure love. There's an absolute knowing of connection and interconnection. Pure unconditional love for everyone there.

What do I do in my days? Seeing myself as a crystal keeper—healing crystal thing—we don't get disease here, so not sure what it is for. To send healing to other places, to Earth and other planets. When I run energy here as Lisa, I am being sent that energy from Arcturus—one of healing lines that I'm tapped into. There's no need for eating in this form. Everything is done in a state of pure joy. Easier to be excited in that state. Optimistic. Wonderment.

What do they want me to know from this place? I have that constant access from that healing energy from that place. I'm here today to remember that so I can move forward and tap into that anytime I need it. To remember that joy and pure love, so when I'm observing things on Earth, it's coming from love, not judgment. Seeing things from the higher perspective. All meant to be playing its part. Even the duality. I can understand what its greater purpose is. They love me."

Channeled message from Uluru, via Lisa, during Ascension session with Tracie:

"Uluru, why did you bring Tracie and Lisa together? We want Lisa to know that she is not alone in this experience. There are others that she can connect with. That she feels solid. That we are really here with her. We have a team here; there are others of us, Arcturians, Zetas, Mantis, Pleiadians, but the We that we speak of is mostly the Arcturian collective.

We are her family. When she met us, she knew immediately that she had been there with us and is still there in a parallel life with us. She's volunteered to come here to Earth to help spread our message of love and unity. It's taken her a while to wake up to that. As she wakes up, it is going to come easier and easier. We are here for her all the time. There are no limitations.

When she works with you, will she channel? Yes, we do see that it will be that way as well as written form.

Does she speak a language or just use hands? She has the ability to use her voice. Can we have a conversation with you right now in Light Language? She's feeling resistant. Not to be afraid. This will clear energy in body. Think about the root chakra and then all the way up to crown— then speak quickly. Feels good to move the energy from tail bone up.

What is the symbol on right palm? Vortex spiral—that's the way to travel dimensions, time and space.

How does that serve me? To get answers from higher places, dimensions, other realities that aren't of Earth. Helps give direction in terms of sharing with people, sharing information, possibly helping them to answer their questions. Expand mind out into infinite possibilities. Just let it flow into me—instantaneous healing and manifestation.

No more stress, no more worry. See the blue Light Language writing moving through my body – I'm not here to be stressed. Looks similar to music notes.

What is around your wrist? Restraint or decoration? Decoration. What do they do for me? Activate the pressure points in wrist—energy flows.

Left hand—whitish-yellow energy for healing. Healing of any disease in body—DNA repair = for me and other people. Take the left hand on third eye—ask yellow energy to heal through mind of thinking it could get ill. Mind knows that is true. What do I want to do with it?

I am bright like the sun. Focus energy on myself. Crown chakra is wide open. When Earth is healed, its vibration is pure love, harmony, peace. There's plenty for everyone. No need for war or jealousy. Everything is connected, and all things know they are connected."

In all of my personal experiences with the Arcturians and hearing the channeling of them through other people, their message is consistent. We are love. We are all connected, unified. I am here to restore balance in the world as a fulcrum. I am here to connect people with higher dimensional beings. I am here to remind people they create their reality. The higher dimensional beings, including the Arcturians, are here to help us.

Chapter 4
Other Cosmic Experiences

"The awakening is the purpose. The awakening of the fact that, in essence, we are light, we are love. Each cell of our body, each cell and molecule of everything. The power source that runs all life is light. So, to awaken to that knowledge, and to desire to operate in that realm, and to believe that it is possible, are all factors that will put you there."
— Dolores Cannon, The Convoluted Universe, Book

Throughout my life, I have had some truly extraordinary experiences in the physical realm as well as the astral realm. The work I have done in the field of past life regression has opened me up to an entirely new way of looking at how the Universe operates. Nothing I have experienced in this life has lacked purpose. It all gives me greater wisdom to step fully into who and what I am.

Visiting Sedona for the First Time

About five years ago, I took the family on vacation during spring break to Sedona, Arizona. Before the trip, I had an energy clearing session with my friend, Colleen. During the session, something came up in the clearing she was a little confused by. It had to do with clearing and deleting alien implants and related things attached to me. She confirmed my connection to entities not of the Earth.

Colleen was confused about the information coming up regarding the alien stuff in our session, as it had not come up in any of our previous sessions. I told her about our pending trip to Sedona and that I had signed us up to go on a UFO tour. This revelation put it all into perspective for her.

Once we were in Sedona, we met the guide for the UFO tour. She taught us all about how to identify what is known in the night sky in terms of the behavior of light and movement. She explained about the energy the crafts give off and the different colors the energy puts out.

Before we were fully set up, several of us, including me and my son, saw a glowing orange orb low on the horizon not far from where we were standing. I knew immediately this was a spacecraft, and our guide confirmed what we saw.

Once it was dark enough, we were able to look through the advanced military night vision goggles. At first, we saw the identified objects and their behavior, including airplanes, satellites, and meteorites. Once we got used to those objects, we were able to see some truly unusual behavior. We watched the night sky and could see a specific portal where ships were leaving without explanation.

I already knew spacecraft and alien visitors were real, but to see this activity in such great quantity was amazing and transformational. It was another layer of experience. This inspired my husband and me to start our own UFO tour company in Hawaii when we arrived, with our own experiences and information.

Moving to Hawaii and the Passion of Pele

In May of 2020, early in the Covid pandemic, I was sitting at the dinner table with my family, and my teenage daughter mentioned she really wanted to move away from Olympia, perhaps to California. Immediately, I got a strong no for California, but without thinking, out of my mouth came, "I would move to Hawaii." My husband was surprised, but he also very quickly said, "I'd move to Hawaii." And thus it began. There was something unknown pulling us to Hawaii like a magnet.

I had only been to the Big Island of Hawaii about eight years before with my former husband and to Maui four years before with my current husband. I knew I had an affinity for the resident manta rays, and I had already met my Polynesian warrior guide during a meditative journey when I was in past life regression training.

The move happened quickly, with a clear path ahead. We made an offer on our new house in September of 2020, closed on it in November, and moved the family at the end of December. When we arrived, I knew this was my home. My understanding of why we were brought here began to unfold. The energy of Hawaii, particularly the Big Island, is vortex-like, similar to the energy of Sedona. The veil is much thinner here.

In reflection, I realized I had met Goddess Pele on the same night I met my Arcturian family in a psychic intuition class

I was taking. As part of the class, we pulled a card from an oracle deck and without looking at it, we were to feel into and see in our mind's eye what was on the card. The card felt warm, and I saw a glowing energy with a woman standing on top of a mountain. When it was time to flip the card over, I saw Pele. The message on the card was, "Be honest with yourself. What is your heart's true desire?"

Although it took a few years from the night of meeting Pele and the Arcturians to really understand what my passion was, I know I have arrived at my purpose being here in Hawaii. Pele reminds me I'm here to help bridge the concept of the goddesses and gods throughout the world being galactic beings. She has told me she put me specifically in the geographic location we are in. She and my other galactic guides are guiding me in this direction of teaching about the galactic realm. Although Hawaii is a naturally active hotspot for UFO activity, the spacecraft are showing up consistently for me the more I am working with them.

Channeled message regarding my connection to Pele during Ascension session with Tracie:

"How do I know her? She's a part of who I am. What is my connection to the volcanoes? Energetically they help build up energy and release it for the earth.

Am I dragon keeper? Yes. How many dragons under my command? A bunch—444. Do the dragons reside in volcanoes? Some do; mine do. When I activate all the dragons, what will happen? Pressure is being released, constriction is gone—fear itself is released.

Who am I? Source energy. I am more than source energy. I am the master keeper of the keepers of the light. I am a master energy and hold the power to the keys and power to dragon realms and to realms of light, all the spectrums, all the colors. I am placed on this planet to help gauge energy and flux of energy to the people and planet because they can't handle the energy. If the energy is too strong, it will kill the people. I help keep the frequencies in check like the wall (in Egypt) was doing for me."

Connection With Inner Earth

When I was a teenager attending the Ramtha School of Enlightenment, I first learned about the beings of Inner Earth. We were taught there was a whole other world inside our planet. Mainstream science says this can't be possible, but there are numerous people who have experienced this world. Navy Admiral Richard E. Byrd was one such person who shared his experience of traveling inside Inner Earth on one of his expeditions to Antarctica. The northern and southern poles are portals going to Inner Earth. There are various gateways and tunnels around the world to access this realm as well.

In my ascension session with Tracie, we got clarity on my particular connection with Inner Earth. Before the channeled and trance portion of the session started, she received information that I had a connection to the violet flame of St. Germaine, as she did. During the session, we explored this more.

Channeled message regarding St. Germaine and Inner Earth during Ascension session with Tracie:

"Can dragon take me to St. Germaine—how am I connected to the purple? Lemurian connection—higher spiritual connection like Lemurians had—connection with Pleiadians, probably other groups. See other groups—Blue Avians. What kind of work do I do with them?

Connected to Ka Aree, Inner Earth beings. There is a tunnel that runs between Mt. Shasta and the Big Island. I work with her. We travel through tunnels, on same circuits, same channels, council members. I am one of her counterparts on the top side. She is part of Telos, Pleiadians, Nordics—I am part of them. I am their informant. I report to them the energy shifts that are happening. Telepathically communicate to her. Thin, tall woman, white hair, blue eyes. She is the soft one, whispers to me. She gathers information telepathically and energetically. We have agreement to do that. She uses that to balance energy in Inner Earth. I can do this on conscious level now. I travel with my dragon to go there. Connections to space—ships that come in and out. I am sensitive to ships that come in and out. Through water, not far from me. How many entry points to enter into Inner Earth? Three points around our island. Have they taken me? I don't have conscious memories. Yes, I have gone there. I wouldn't want to come back if I was conscious.

Step into certainty. When I do it for people, I am more certain. Why do I hold doubt for myself? Fear that I am extraordinary. I am beyond extraordinary, amazing. Doesn't mean better than. When I hold doubt for myself, I put that on others. I will step in fully to my knowingness, certainty. Stepping into the knowing that this energy can be beneficial to the Earth. I am going to embody this vibration and this frequency, and the people that are ready to understand it will come to me. I will not attract those that want to be special. Everyone on this planet has the special ability. That is what I am awakening them to. Everyone is special. I help people see things so much differently. I do it with own spin, uniqueness.

Bring the Inner Earth journey for my people, and it will help me remember. Take them into the tunnels to experience Pele and the other beings."

Exploring My Life as a Mermaid From Sirius

In the same ascension session with Tracie, I wanted to explore one of my lives on Sirius. I was living on a planet with merpeople. I could see myself swimming in the water with them. I realized I was a mermaid—I was one of them. It was so beautiful under the water, with so many beautiful colors and textures.

Channeled message from Mermaid Life during Ascension session with Tracie:

"Life is easy there. There isn't hard work. Everything is just right there. There's compassion and love. How do I feel swimming? Easy and fun, much better than Earth body. There's communion with whales and dolphins here. They are friends. Communicate with them easily. Where do I live? Seeing an underwater cave. Cozy. Feels like for

resting the body, not for staying in there all day. When I'm in that body, what does it feel like? Sleek, longer, more streamlined for the water. Feels very muscular, especially the tail, strong muscles for swimming. Very graceful—grace and power."

Ancient Egypt and the Sirian Connection

In my ascension session with Tracie, the first experience that came up was a connection to Ancient Egypt. At the time, it wasn't completely clear what my role in this time and place was. Sometime after the session, when I was having a conversation with my friend, Lee, I received a clear message I was actually a Sirian being interacting *with* Egypt, rather than being one of the Egyptians. I was part of the genetic modification process of the human body, a Sirian genetic engineer.

Another interesting tidbit of information I learned after this session is that Sirian energy is used for physical healing of the body, whereas Arcturian energy is used for emotional healing. The following channeling alludes to the physical healing connection with light, as well as using sound. I recently was called to become certified in *sound healing* to add to my healing toolbox.

Channeled message regarding Ancient Egypt during Ascension session with Tracie:

"Energy that pyramids create is connection to source energy. Bring the Egyptian life into my mind. Seeing inside pyramid. Dark energy that I'm coming up against—feels

like a wall that I can't go through. It needs light shown on it. What is purpose for being there? To slow me down. Why? Too much power, too fast. Thank you, wall, for being there, but now I don't need it. Ask the wall to carry the bright lights—yes—can see light all around—deep gold color.

Tunnel—can see the path down, glowing—walked through tunnel and now surrounded by pure white light—that's where all the answers can be found—I can go there anytime I want/need—I have that availability.

Doubts, fears, belief systems getting in my way of remembering. Gifted, talented, how fast I am—remember. I am activating the planet—restructuring crystal grids on Earth—I am here to help and orchestrate that.

What can I do with the light? I can expand out that energy beyond my house—it's part of the healing—my body is so much lighter—I am beyond the earth somewhere out in space—now in the multiverse space—layers of dimensions—the void.

Advice for Lisa—know that I have access to everything that I need to do the work I am doing. There are no limitations. Doubts can be overcome in a second. Everything is possible.

Physical body being healed instantly in this moment—my body being absorbed in this light.

Blockage in the palm of right hand. Use left hand to heal. Use pitch—tingles—I can feel vibration of sound through my body."

Additional Galactic Connections

In addition to my connections with the Arcturians, Sirians, Inner Earth beings, and my group from Io, other Galactic entities have interacted with me in various ways.

After meeting my Arcturian family during the first night of the psychic class, I experienced Andromedans and Blue Avians in the second class of the series. Their message to me was I was a transmitter of peace. My self-acceptance lights the way. My natural peace heals others.

The Andromedans showed up for me in a pyramid-shaped craft on 2/22/22, which was a powerful portal day. I had gathered with a group of like-minded people at my friend Brittany's house in Hawaii and led them through a meditative journey to activate their DNA, raise their vibration, and call in spacecraft. During the journey, it was pouring down rain. Although the rain stopped shortly after, the sky was completely covered with clouds, so we wouldn't be able to use the night vision goggles.

My husband and I were walking up the driveway to where the car was parked when we saw a giant outline of an upright pyramid/triangle in the clouds. The lines were so sharp there was no way it could have been a different light source. I knew it was a ship. We met up with Brittany, and she had observed the same thing. The three of us were the only ones to see it in the group. Later, I got confirmation from my friend Lee that it was the Andromedans saying hi.

The Blue Avians have come up a few times in different sessions, but I have not yet connected all of the dots as to my experience with them.

Another galactic group that has been showing up a lot in the last year for me is the Mantis beings. They have come physically to me several times in the form of praying mantis insects, clearly in my line of vision and path. They have also come through my sessions with Lee and Tracie with the message I have roots in the Mantis collective. They represent the Divine Masculine Energy. They are highly evolved beings, master geneticists and master healers. I have felt their healing energy during the night when I am sleeping. I have met with them in my dreams.

DNA Activation Leads to Light Language and More

Before moving to Hawaii, I had never heard of Light Language. My first experience of it was at a Full Moon Ceremony I attended soon after the move. One of my new friends on the island felt compelled to share her Light Language with the group at the end of the ceremony. Although the words did not make any sense, I could feel the energy vibration of the syllables. My body tingled. After the experience, my friend shared her Light Language a few more times in my presence. Other people were coming across my path who also spoke Light Language, in addition to writing it and using their hands.

In the fall of 2021, I received a DNA activation that completely changed my energy. The next day, my hands started moving on their own, with sort of a dancing and sign language type of expression. I quickly realized this was a form of Light Language. As I moved my hands, I could feel the energy of my body shifting and tingling, similar to the way the spoken Light Language had made me feel. I now have the ability to do this on-demand, and I use it in my healing sessions with my clients, as well as on myself. The vocalization and writing of Light Language are beginning to come through me.

This was the first step toward being a vocal channel. The more work I do with connecting to my galactic family and guides, the more they desire to work and speak through me to share their empowering messages. I am learning to step aside and trust the process. I am so much more than this Earth human Lisa. I am a cosmic force in the Universe.

Chapter 5
Being a Tourist on Planet Earth

*"We must never forget that we chose to be here,
and we are here for a reason."*
— Dolores Cannon, The Search for Hidden, Sacred
Knowledge

Have you ever wondered why you decided to incarnate on the Earth plane? I have wondered that myself so many times throughout my life. Earth is hard. It's dense. It's rife with polarity, war, and disease. Most humans are living their lives "asleep" and unaware of who they are and where they came from. They forget why they chose to be here.

In the work I've done on myself, I have made some realizations about how I came to be Lisa, living this Earth existence. I know I chose my parents to learn lessons of self-love and worthiness. The challenging situations I have experienced in my life stemming from those early relationships with my parents have transmuted into much wisdom. This allows me to feel compassion and empathy for others who feel stuck in their situation in a way I did not before I went through tough times myself. It has helped me to identify patterns where I was recreating toxic experiences with different people. I got myself out of the cycle. My light can shine the way for others to get out of their patterns and limiting belief systems.

I chose my mother specifically to be able to remember who I really am at a higher level early in life, rather than having to be asleep my entire life. Even with this information, I rebelled and had to do it my way for a long time. It was much easier to come back to it when I was ready. I am thankful I did not have religious programming I had to undo like my mother and so many of my friends. I grew up knowing I create my reality—I am one with the Universe—I am Source.

The following are some of the reasons why I am here at this time and in this place. These are the things I love about this Earth experience.

My Love of Animals

I have always loved animals of all kinds. As a child, I was obsessed with them. I learned everything I could about them. I would spend hours drawing them. I loved seeing animals in zoos and aquariums, which I otherwise would not have been able to experience living in Oklahoma as a child. I love observing animals in their natural habitats and seeing how they live. My passion turned into my first career as a zoologist and marine biologist.

When I was around the age of nine, I read a book about Eugenie Clark, *The Shark Lady*. She was a pioneer female biologist studying sharks back in the 1960s and onward. I decided I wanted to follow her path because I thought sharks were misunderstood, and I wanted to learn about them and teach people to overcome their fear of the animals.

When it was time to decide what I would study for my dissertation in graduate school, I settled on studying the batoid fishes—the flat sharks—which includes the skates, stingrays, manta rays and their relatives. There was even less known about them than the traditional sharks, and I loved how much diversity there was in shape and behavior in the group.

My dissertation was titled, *The Evolution of Batoid Locomotion*. It combined the fields of functional morphology, evolutionary relationships, and fluid biomechanics. It was fascinating to learn about how these animals adapted their behavior and shape to their environment. Their disc shapes resemble different types of spacecraft, including the stealth bomber.

In working with live specimens, I got to know them personally. They each had distinctive personalities. The more I studied them, the more I loved them.

Later, I had the opportunity to swim with the giant manta rays and continue to do so regularly now that I live in Hawaii, where they live year-round. Mantas are the most highly evolved of all the fishes. They have the largest brain of any fish in the world, even larger than the whale shark. They are gentle giants who have lost their stinging spine, and they don't have teeth as they eat plankton. They are higher dimensional sentient beings in a physical third-dimensional body.

In addition to my deep dive study into the shark family, I have also had the opportunity to learn a great deal about other marine and terrestrial animals. As a university professor, I taught marine biology and zoology. I loved

CONNECTION TO THE COSMOS

being able to share about the vast biodiversity we have here on Earth.

As an adult, I've made a point of doing eco-tourism, where I have been able to experience animals in their natural habitat. This has included visiting Australia, Africa, Thailand, Mexico, and Belize.

We often put humans on an evolutionary pedestal, but we could learn so much by understanding animals and the capacity they have to love. Loving and appreciating different kinds of life forms on our planet allows us to be more open to when we experience other forms of life that are not of this Earth or of this dimension. I embrace diversity.

Appreciating Food & Drink

Recently I had a mild case of Covid, which I identified immediately upon losing my taste and smell. While the loss only lasted a week, it made me appreciate the taste of food and drink, which is truly yummy, and the smell of amazing aromas.

I didn't have as much of an appetite and interest in eating food when I couldn't taste it. This was better for my waistline but not for my enjoyment of life. I love the variety of foods from different cultures, particularly Thai, Indian, and sushi. I enjoy a really bold red wine, a cup of great coffee or Chai tea, and dark chocolate. I love fresh organic vegetables.

At higher dimensional levels, there is no need to eat food for energy the way we need it here on Earth. This goes back to the physical body we live in. We get to experience a plethora of flavors, bringing pleasure to our sensory systems.

As our energy vibration increases, moving from third dimension to fifth dimension, the more our bodies are lightening, which reduces our desire for heavier food. At some point, you may find yourself craving more and more plant material over animal material for sustenance, as has happened to me. You may already be there. Take time to really enjoy the flavors and smells of the food you take into the body.

Diversity of Cultures and Land

I love the beauty of planet Earth—the colors, textures, and diversity of life and environments. I relish being in beautiful interior environments. I love what nature has to offer. I love the diversity of the human form. There is so much beauty all around.

I have always loved learning about and exploring other cultures from around the world. There are some I immediately resonated with and had a knowing I had some affiliation.

The first country I was obsessed with as a child was Australia. The animals were my favorite, and I loved learning about the land and the people. It wasn't until seven years ago I got to visit. It was like coming home. I knew I had been there before. About four years ago, I was in a past life regression session with my teacher, Denise Linn, and I got to experience one of my lives as a young male Aborigine on walkabout. The connections the Aborigines have with the land, the animals, and the star people are very much a part of who I am as Lisa.

India is another place of fascination for me. In grade school, one of my teachers would share stories about her travels to India. I had the opportunity to learn about Hinduism in eighth grade for a school project. I love the food, the bright colors, the dancing, and the design elements. My first husband is of Indian descent (and had grown up in Australia). One of my spirit guides is an Indian priestess.

Five years ago, I had the opportunity to discover my connection and embodiment of the Hindu Goddess, Saraswati. She is the Goddess of knowledge, music, art, wisdom, science and higher learning. She represents light, knowledge and truth. Her name is translated as the "One Who Flows." She is called upon to help manifest thoughts, dreams and passions. She invokes a flow of energy in the dreamer and artist, allowing the creative life force to flow within. She inspires.

Traveling to Mexico and Belize to experience the Mayan culture is always amazing for me. The energy permeating the areas of the Mayan ruins is undeniable. Walking through the different sites brought back visions of being there in one form or another. The galactic connection is strong with the Mayan people, as they are said to be physically embodied from Sirius.

The first time I visited Hawaii ten years ago, I knew it was a special place beside the resident population of manta rays. Now that I live here, I more fully understand my connection to this land. It is part of the remnant of the lost continent of Lemuria, which spanned from Easter Island to

Hawaii and throughout Polynesia, Indonesia, and Micronesia down to New Zealand. It has strong vortex energy, which is great for revealing and healing blockages. The Big Island is home to Goddess Pele, one of my other embodiments. The first spirit guide I met was a Polynesian warrior. The Big Island is one of the access points to Inner Earth and has a strong connection to Arcturus and the Pleiades.

Egypt is another place I resonate with, although I have not yet made the trek there in this life. In the last few months, I have come to understand my connection to Ancient Egypt in a deeper way. The Sirians (beings from Sirius) were one of the groups who genetically modified the human species to be able to carry more energy in their bodies. I was/am one of these beings involved in the genetic project as a genetic engineer.

These are just a few of the places I have experienced in this life. I love to travel, and I truly appreciate the diversity of people on this planet. Even though we are made up of all different shapes, sizes, and colors, we are all one human race. We are all united. The more we can appreciate our differences and our similarities, the faster we will move to fifth dimensional reality. It's time to come together in unity. The more we can accept others, the better able we are going to be in welcoming in life, not of Earth.

Sexual Relations

One of the true pleasures of being in a third dimensional human body is experiencing sensual and sexual relations. I love having sex and being intimate with my husband.

Because of the trust and respect we have, we share a level of intimacy I have not experienced with anyone else in this life. The sensations in my body and mind are intense. I can feel his energy integrating with mine. Our two bodies become one energetically. Sometimes I can feel what he is feeling in his body—his pleasure. I regularly have flashbacks to other "lives" we are simultaneously living, and I joke about us being contributing authors to the Kama Sutra. This goes back to my affinity toward the land of India.

To experience this level of pleasure, I believe it is imperative one heals any sexual trauma they have encountered in this (or other) life. Being able to really trust someone and open up to them at a soul level requires a form of vulnerability that is not necessarily easy or common. Carefully choose who you let into your intimate life if you want to have this deeper sexual connection I describe.

At higher dimensional levels, sex is not important as the physical body is very different or even non-existent. I know I came here to experience the pleasures of the physical body. In this day and time, we live in a world where we can freely have sexual relations without the stigma some of the other time periods have had.

Teaching

It's interesting no matter what I have done in my life for work or hobby, I have continually been a teacher in those areas. As a teenager, I was a dancer and choreographer and taught dance at a dance studio and to my high school dance team. In the field of biology, I was a professor at the college level. In the mortgage industry, I taught homeowners how to pay off their home loans significantly faster by using their money in smarter ways via workshops, one-on-one consulting, and through a book I wrote. As an interior designer, I taught at home shows, through writing regular articles for the local newspaper, and via my book, *Sacred Soul Spaces: Designing Your Personal Oasis*.

Now, as a spiritual teacher and healer, I am teaching inspired knowledge to those who want to learn and practice. These topics include Human Design, self-love and worthiness (via my book, *Sacred Soul Love: Manifesting True Love and Happiness by Revealing and Healing Blockages and Limitations*), past/parallel lives, galactic consciousness, the Universe, and more. I love sharing my experiences and wisdom with others. I am compelled to share my knowledge in whatever way I can.

Living My Earth Life to Its Fullest

So here I am, living a fully embodied human life in the three-dimensional world and moving to the fifth dimension. I choose to love this physical expression and the expansion and contraction in size, shape and form. It's all beautiful. I'm a huge energy in a little package of the body. I am here to express myself. I am here to experience pleasure. I am here to gain wisdom and then share it. I am here to shine my light.

Although I have many more embodiments off planet Earth, here I am being Lisa, enjoying Hawaii, having fun, and opening curiosity. The Council of Light Beings, who helped me plan this incarnation, reminded me a few months ago of why I chose to come in as Lisa and have challenging experiences. It was so that when I remembered who and what I am and was able to heal myself, I would have compassion, empathy and love for other Earth humans. I am here to be a light so people don't stay stuck. By me going through my darkness and transmuting it, I'm a wayshower helping others transmute their darkness. Life doesn't have to be hard, just fun.

I fully appreciate that I am becoming more and more aware of my powers and abilities. My connection with my galactic family and my spirit guides helps me to know I am not alone on this journey. I have an army of support around me, including my Polynesian warrior, Indian priestess, Ascended Masters (St. Germaine, Yeshua ben Joseph, and Apollonius of Tianna), a team of dragons, Uluru (my Arcturian family), Mantis beings, Tall Whites, Angels, Fairies, Goddesses (Saraswati and Pele), Inner Earth Beings, Light Beings, and so many more. They are here to protect and guide me in and out of situations that can be harmful and to give me ideas of which direction to take. I am all of them, and so are you.

Journal Prompt: Think about all of the things you appreciate about your own experience of being a tourist on Earth. List them here. It's important to remember some of the reasons we chose to be in this Earth incarnation at this time.

SECTION 2: UNDERSTANDING UFO AND ALIEN PHENOMENA

Chapter 6
Understanding Terminology in the UFO Paradigm

"Quantum theory tells us, Mr. Thomas, that every point in the universe is intimately connected to every other point, regardless of apparent distance. In some mysterious way, any point on a planet in a distant galaxy is as close to me as you are."
— Dean Koontz, Brother Odd

In order to understand the reality of visitation from beyond our Earth time and space, it is important to have a common set of vocabulary to discuss. The terminology I use may be different from what other authors use, so I want to be clear in my explanations. Feel free to interchange your terminology with how I am describing things.

UFOs, UAPs, and USOs

In the UFO community, there has been a recent change in how spacecraft are referred to in the mass media and among military and government officials. *Flying saucer* was the original coined term, first used by Kenneth Arnold after he saw spacecraft over Mt. Rainier shaped like saucers in 1947. The term *unidentified flying object* (UFO), replaced the term flying saucer in the 1950s. The study of this phenomenon became known as Ufology.

The newer term being used in the media and government is *unidentified aerial phenomena* (UAP). In 2020, the Department of Defense approved the creation of the Unidentified Aerial Phenomena Task Force to catalog and study UAPs. Using UAP over UFO is seen by some, including myself, as a way to avoid popular connotations of UFOs. In my mind, there really was no need to change the name, and I prefer using UFO to refer to alien spacecraft.

There is also the term *unidentified submerged object* (USO). These are unexplained objects in the water. Some of the objects which have been seen and videoed move between the air and water easily and are referred to as transmedium craft.

Extraterrestrial, Extradimensional, and Interdimensional

When most people think of alien life, they tend to use the term *extraterrestrial* (ET). Extraterrestrial simply means originating from outside of Earth's atmosphere and being from space or another planet.

In the more nuanced study of Ufology, aliens can be categorized as *extradimensional* (ED), where they originate outside the known physical reality of the universe. These beings reside in a higher dimension and density. The extradimensional beings may reside in the Earth realm, and they may also reside in other locations.

Some of the beings who visit us on Earth are truly extraterrestrial but still have a physical reality to them, which we can see at our dense Earth vibration. Some reside on Earth but at such a higher vibration that we cannot see their physical form. Other beings are both extraterrestrial and extradimensional simultaneously.

The term *interdimensional* (ID) is sometimes used to refer to other beings as well. Interdimensional is defined as existing or traveling between dimensions of time or space. In the science fiction world, it is commonly used to refer to something coming from an alternate dimension or parallel universe.

When the word *alien* is used in the Ufology community, it refers to something foreign, not from this place. It has a more generic meaning of not originating from this Earth and also not from the third dimension. The term alien actually can encompass all of the extraterrestrials, extra-dimensionals, and interdimensionals, so this is how I will be referring to non-Earth humans in this book.

The distinction of different forms aliens can take is important when we are talking about the existence of life in the Universe. Mainstream science has a limited, narrow-minded view of what life is. The scientific paradigm wants to measure it, see it, touch it, and experience it with our five main senses. What I have come to understand is there is third dimension physical life on other planets, but there is so much more residing in the higher dimensions and realities that science doesn't have the tools or techniques to measure at this point in time.

Dimensions Versus Densities

When talking about different forms of life, the use of the terms *dimensions* and *densities* are commonly inter-changed. Instead of thinking of dimensions and densities as different places, rather they can all exist simultaneously in the same space. Densities refer to the physical aspect of the dimensions. When we are talking about dimensions, we are referring to how it is vibrating. As something vibrates faster and faster, it experiences higher dimensions, and the density becomes less physical.

As an example, imagine the blades of a fan. When the fan is turned off, you can visibly see each individual blade. As the fan gets turned on and goes faster, the individual blades are now indistinguishable. They are vibrating at a faster rate—a higher frequency. The turned-off fan demonstrates a denser reality, one vibrating at a lower frequency.

7 Densities and their Vibrational Expression

Atoms and molecules, the building blocks of life, reside in 1st density reality.

Minerals, plants, and some animals reside in 2nd density, where they share a group or species identity. They do not possess self-awareness. They vibrate at a 3rd dimensional rate, which is how they appear solid to us.

We as humans are currently existing in a 3rd density awareness, with a vibration experience of 3rd and 4th dimensions. Because we are vibrating on this level, we are able to see and experience other things vibrating at a similar frequency. In this reality, we still have a physical body, and we experience polarity in our world. We are aware of ourselves as individuals, which creates an illusion of separation. We also experience the illusion of time through past, present, and future experiences due to the vibration being slow.

In 4th density, 5th dimensional reality, there is still a physical body present, although it is less dense. There is no longer polarization of the lower levels. The concept of time becomes more fluid where times exist simultaneously. The individual ego can exist, as well as the experience of being part of a collective. This is the beginning place of instant manifestation and creating reality in real-time. Fairies are an example of an Earth-based group residing in 4th density. When people talk about us moving from 3rd dimension to 5th dimension, they are referring to this experience of having 4th density reality.

In the 5th density, 6th dimensional experience, the physical body disappears, so there is a non-physical orientation. There is more of a collective expression while still having some individual expression able to come through. Linear time does not exist in this realm.

The reality of 6th density with 7th dimensional vibration (and higher) expresses as a pure energy light body in non-physical form. It is Christ and Buddha consciousness where one fully remembers who and what they are. It is awareness of the dimension itself.

As we move to 7th density, it becomes the frequency of total integration where awareness is experienced as multidimensional. It is said this is the final step before we move into a new adventure in a different reality or universe.

Whether referring to dimension or density, it is important to note there is a continuum between the different subcategories just described, moving from a lower to a higher state of vibration within each level. We label them as different levels for our brain to comprehend the concept better, but in reality, there are no distinct boundary lines set in stone. Some beings are multidimensional and have the ability to reside in the density of their choosing for a particular expression or experience.

Now that we have defined densities and dimensions, we can understand there are aliens we experience at these different levels. When a channeled "collective" refers to what dimension they reside in, it is an imaginary number meant to refer to what frequency they vibrate at.

Higher Dimensional Beings

Just as there are higher dimensional beings living among us on Earth and inside of Earth, some of the other groups of aliens have representatives from different dimensions. The higher dimensions can observe their dimension and all the dimensions below them. So, for instance, a Pleiadian vibrating at 12th dimension is going to have more information and connection to direct source than a Pleiadian residing in 6th dimension.

Some of these higher dimensional beings have the ability to lower their vibration to a level that can be experienced by some of the lower levels, including taking on a physical form. Likewise, we as humans have the ability to increase our vibration to connect with higher dimensional beings. There are stories throughout our history where certain people have been able to increase their vibration to appear invisible and walk through walls. Apollonius of Tianna, a contemporary of Jesus, has been documented as becoming invisible and disappearing in a Roman courtroom.

During the temporary detainment experiences where humans are said to float through ceilings and walls, their frequency vibrates fast enough that their bodies are no longer solid compared to the three-dimensional structure they are passing through. Our bodies are not solid. We are 99% empty space.

I mentioned earlier that fairies reside in the 4th density, 5th dimensional realm. They coexist with us here on Earth; therefore, they are not extraterrestrial, but they are extradimensional. Some people have the vision to experience them physically.

When we refer to Ascended Masters, we are talking about higher dimensional beings who lived on Earth at one time and were able to raise their vibration high enough to take their physical body with them. They ascended to a higher level. They were teachers, healers, or wayshowers of ascension. Although we are familiar with Jesus, Buddha and Mohamed, there have been thousands of Ascended Masters throughout time and in all cultures around the world. My former teacher Ramtha, introduced in an earlier chapter, is an Ascended Master. They spread the message of love. They are extradimensional beings.

Angels are higher dimensional beings who have not lived as humans or animals. They haven't incarnated on other planets either, based on most of the teachings I have heard and read. They reside in a higher dimensional realm than the Ascended Masters. For more information on angels, I recommend *Invoking the Archangels: a Nine-step Process to Heal Your Body, Mind, and Soul* by my friend and mentor, Sunny Dawn Johnston.

What's interesting about angels is there is some channeled information saying the Arcturians appear as angels to some people. If someone grows up in a religious household and believes in angels, that is how the Arcturians will appear to them. For those like me, they appear to be more alien in nature. One of my good friends who has channeled the energy of the angels and the Arcturians has shared with me that the energy feels very similar when they are coming through. It's a very high vibration, different than the fairies and the Ascended Masters.

Now that we have common terminology and an understanding of densities and dimensions, we will explore where aliens come from and why they visit us.

Chapter 7
Where Aliens Come From and Why They Visit Us

"There may be aliens in our Milky Way galaxy, and there are billions of other galaxies. The probability is almost certain that there is life somewhere in space."
—Buzz Aldrin

With the understanding you have now of extra-terrestrials and extradimensionals, lumped into a general category of aliens, it becomes easier to talk about where these beings come from and why they are visiting us.

Where Aliens Come From

Aliens come from different locations and dimensions throughout the universe. Based on channeled material, recounts of peoples' personal experiences, and whistle-blower insider information coming out of the government and military-industrial complex, there is intelligent life on most of the planets and some of the moons in our solar system. Some aliens reside right here on Earth, living among us, in our dimensional reality and higher dimensional vibrations. There are beings living inside the Earth, referred to as Agarthans. Other aliens from the planets and moons in our solar system also live underground, such as my group from Io. They typically reside in higher dimensions. Venus is one such planet that has Earth-like humans living underground, vibrating at 5th dimensional frequency.

Aliens come from distant stars and galaxies, such as Orion, Lyra, Sirius, Arcturus, Pleiades, Andromeda, Antares, and many more. Within those systems, there is more than just one species or race. Some of these beings are humanoid in form. Others look completely different. The Pleiades constellation alone has been said to have more than 10,000 intelligent species.

There are galactic beings residing on ships out in space in different dimensions. They travel by changing their dimension, utilizing wormholes, moving backward and forward through time, folding space-time, and other quantum mechanisms. These beings are far more advanced than we are, so they have developed the technology to travel where time and space are not an issue like they are for our current Earth reality.

Some of the spacecraft witnessed within Earth's atmosphere are actually military vehicles that have been reverse-engineered from crashed spacecraft (think Roswell and similar crash sites). It can be difficult to distinguish between what is ours versus what is non-Earth originated.

Why Aliens are Interacting With Earth

There are many alien races visiting Earth, with each having its own specific agenda for the visitation. Some of these races work together for a common cause. UFO activity has been going on since the beginning of life on Earth, with more activity noticed at different periods in time.

Ancient artifacts which defy the level of technology during those time periods have been found around the world in most of the native cultures, supporting the ancient astronaut theory. The stories of the "gods" in different cultures and in religious texts, like the Bible and the Sumerian tablets, point to UFO activity and visitation. Carvings in rock and stone depict the alien visitors. The first 15 seasons of the TV show Ancient Aliens are a good representation of the history of alien visitors throughout time. Erich von Däniken is credited with being one of the first Ancient Astronaut Theorists. His original book, *Chariots of the Gods?*, provides evidence of ancient visitation.

We have up to 22 different alien species intermixed in our DNA. Throughout human evolution, different alien races have come to splice in their DNA, which we'll cover in detail in Chapters 10 and 11. Earth has been an experimental laboratory of sorts. Some of these groups are believed to be here to watch over us, as we are their offspring. Several channeled extradimensional beings from different star systems have said we as Earth humans are unique in having such a mixture of different alien races within us. The purpose of the genetic modifications was to try to create the perfect body, the perfect vehicle. The human experiment on Earth got side-railed when the big meteor hit and brought new strains of bacteria, causing diseases.

Other groups are here for some of the resources on Earth, such as gold and other minerals. Ancient Sumerian texts describe the Anunnaki (translated as "those who from heaven to earth came") coming to Earth to mine gold, which was later written about by author Zecharia Sitchin in his first book, *The 12th Planet*.

There are some Reptilian humanoids who arrived here on Earth well before modern humans evolved, living here for millions of years. Most of them have gone underground to Inner Earth with the remnants of the Lemurians and Atlanteans. They are known to occasionally interact with the surface.

One group of gray aliens, the Zetas, have a soul-level agreement with some Earth humans to develop a hybrid species for the Zetas and Earth humans to be able to reincarnate into. This is part of the temporary detainment experience, which will be explained in Chapters 9 and 10.

Other alien groups take people into their spacecraft and test them off-planet for pollutants in their bodies. We have done so much destruction and polluted the Earth in a huge way. We've polluted our water, our air, and our food. These beings are studying how the pollutants are affecting humans.

Some alien groups interact with specific humans to upgrade or activate their DNA. As our world is evolving, so is the human body. The DNA activation allows our body to hold more energy and vibrate at a higher frequency.

Some groups interact with us to help our bodies heal. They either take the physical body or the astral (etheric) body into their ship. Others visit during sleep and perform the healing while we are in bed. Some of them work on us in our waking state without us being aware of their presence.

CHAPTER 7 | WHERE AILIENS COME FROM AND WHY THEY VISIT US

The development of atomic energy generated a lot of attention from aliens because what we do here on Earth has a very direct impact on the Universe. It creates a ripple effect across space and dimensions. We are an interconnected web of consciousness, so what affects one affects the whole. Some of these groups have been observed around and even active in shutting down nuclear weapons facilities all over the world, which has been disclosed by different military personnel. One such instance occurred at Malmstrom Air Force Base in Montana in 1967. The aliens want to prevent the situation which happened in Atlantis, where the technology became more advanced than the spiritual development of the people. At the time of my journey to Io in the late 1980s, we were on the brink of World War III with the threat of nuclear weapons. We are once again in a precarious situation.

There are aliens monitoring our volcanic activity and possibly helping to control this activity and other weather events, which could create severe devastation. There are many UFO sightings around dormant and active volcanoes around the world. Here in Hawaii on the Big Island, we have the most active volcano in the world, Kilauea, and we have a high amount of UFO activity. There is a lot of activity seen throughout the Cascade Mountains, including Rainier, Adams, and Shasta. An active volcano in Mexico also has a lot of regular activity, as do volcanoes in Iceland.

Some of the alien visitors are thought to be us (either as Earth humans or in other forms), just coming from the past and/or the future. Dr. Michael P. Masters explains this theory in his book, *Identified Flying Objects: A Multidisciplinary Scientific Approach to UFO Pheno-*

menon. Because all timelines exist simultaneously, some advanced beings have the technology to "time" travel. I recently had an experience of visiting myself as my Arcturian self, where I was able to observe my job in that world. I am a healer, but we don't need healing on Arcturus. The healing is sent through a quartz crystal to my Earth self to use on myself and others.

There are 3rd density aliens (still in a vibration of polarity) with advanced technology who are believed to visit with agendas focusing more on service to themselves. Some of these groups are reported to work with various governments, including the U.S. government, advising on science and technology since the 1950s Eisenhower administration. These polarized beings are the ones the media and U.S. government give more attention to because they are perpetuating a fear-based agenda and desire to control the population. There is a Galactic Federation of different alien races actively working to keep these lower dimensional beings off of Earth. This rabbit hole is beyond the scope of this book and my purpose of sharing information on aliens. The beings residing in non-polarity, in the higher dimensions, far outnumber the groups who are still polarized.

My Arcturians really want me to drive home the message that they and other alien groups are here to help us to remember where we came from and how powerful we really are. Love and unity are the true nature of the Universe. As with our disco ball example from earlier, we are all one. We are in the midst of evolving as a species to a higher density and dimension. Some people are not ready for this and are checking out early. Those of us who are ready need to be actively lifting our own vibration on a regular basis to be more in the flow with this change.

In the next chapter, we'll explore different kinds of interactions humans have with alien visitors.

Chapter 8
Interactions With Aliens

"Look at the stars... It helps you to remember that you and your problems are both infinitesimally small and, conversely, that you are a piece of an amazing and vast universe."
— Kate Bartolotta

It's important to understand the numerous ways in which interactions with aliens occur. The majority of people would likely expect it to be a physical, 3rd density experience where a craft is seen with the naked eye and an alien being is standing in front of them. While this is possible, it is not the way most interactions happen. In this chapter, we will explore the different states of interactions, types of interactions based on the *Close Encounters Scale*, and observing spacecraft and orbs.

Different States of Interactions

Our human brain has a range of activities from wide awake to very deep sleep, which allows us to experience and remember things at a variety of levels. This relates directly to the frequency at which we vibrate and the dimension we experience.

Beta - When we are fully awake and conscious of what is around us, we are in a beta brainwave state. This is experiencing a 3rd dimensional reality.

Alpha - In the daydreaming state, known as alpha, our consciousness experiences more of a 4th dimensional reality where we can see things others can't see that are in the beta state.

Theta - Theta state is just before sleep, in deep relaxation. At this level, we can experience 4th and 5th dimensional reality.

Delta - Deep sleep is known as delta, where we access 4th and 5th dimensional experience. This includes lucid dreaming, where we can control and change our dreams.

Because the majority of the aliens who are interacting with us reside in a higher dimension, most of the experiences people have with them are in alpha, theta, and delta states. The beta state is too dense and slow for most of the aliens to interact. The higher dimensional aliens have so much energy that our body naturally goes into one of these three dream states when we are in their presence. So even if a ship were to land right in front of us, most people would go into a trance-like state immediately.

There are some alien groups residing in a 4th and 5th density reality with the ability to lower their vibration to 3rd density existence in short moments, but it is hard for them to maintain because it is so dense and slow. Some of the higher dimensional beings can fluctuate their vibration to be multidimensional. The majority of aliens who exist in the universe are in 4th density reality and above.

Our human sensory system is limited in what it can experience. As an example, our eyes can only see a portion of the light spectrum, which we call visible, but animals like cats can see infrared. Our ears can only detect a small range of the sound frequencies available, but dogs can hear outside of our range. Our bodies vibrate within a range of frequencies as well.

When we raise our vibration, we increase our frequency, which gives us an altered perspective and the ability to experience higher dimensions. This is how we are able to perceive objects like spacecraft and alien entities residing in higher frequencies.

Any entities who exist outside (i.e., above or below) the frequency range we vibrate at will not be visible to our eyes and can therefore be said to exist in a "different dimension" (i.e., extradimensional). In order to see form in this dimension, humans would need to raise their vibration and/or the higher dimensional entities would need to lower their vibration to a position where there is overlap.

We can actively put ourselves into these states to initiate a connection with aliens, which we will cover in Chapters 14 and 15. The Aborigines of Australia do this in their dreamtime state. Native tribes around the world do this in trance and with medicinal plants.

We have the ability to astral travel, and we often do it without even realizing it. All experiences in our dreams, whether sleeping or daydream state, are real. It's all a real connection and deeper than the physical level. The ego-mind wants to protect itself, so it files those memories in the back of our minds in the subconscious. We can retrieve all of those memories and experiences through deep hypnosis.

Interactions with other beings can be in the physical body, where the physical body raises in high enough vibration to be pulled into a craft (and even through walls if needed). Occasionally people have come back with distinct marks which give physical proof of interaction.

Other interactions with aliens can be out of body experiences where the physical body is still present on Earth, and the astral body travels where needed. They can also happen as channelings of information through your voice, thoughts coming into your head, or through your writing.

A lot of my personal experiences happen in meditative journeys. This is as real as being taken physically. The mind does not know the difference between what we experience with our eyes open versus closed. The internal journeys are profound and allow you to interact with much higher dimensional beings.

A couple of years ago, I had a thought cross my mind, which came again last year, regarding mental psychoses. When someone is labeled with a mental disorder, such as schizophrenia, and is experiencing other people and beings visually or audibly who those around them cannot see or hear, those experiences are real. They are tapping into other dimensions. Western culture and psychiatric medicine do not understand this the way a lot of native cultures do.

For those of you who want to have a connection, meditation is an excellent gateway to this. Have the intent and trust you can connect. One of the things I need to make you aware of if you are new to this is you really need to work on your fears and clear out the monsters of your mind. Shine light in the dark spaces. Train your mind to embrace diversity of form and shape. We tend to fear the unknown as humans, so when we see something that looks unusual, it can produce a fear response, even if the situation is completely neutral or benevolent. Also, know you have free will and are fully in control over situations occurring in your life. The more work you do with your shadow self, the better experiences you will have in these meditative and dream-like states.

Types of Interactions – the Close Encounters Scale

In 1972, Dr. J. Allen Hynek from Project Bluebook created a scale to help identify activity and visitation by aliens. His Close Encounters (CE) Scale was published in *The UFO Experience: A Scientific Inquiry*. His scale is based on the assumption of only 3rd density experiences.

Close Encounter 1: Visual sightings less than 500 feet away showing considerable detail.

Close Encounter 2: A UFO event in which a physical effect is alleged, such as a vehicle turning on and off unexplainably, electronics going haywire, animals (including mutilation), visual evidence on a person's body, and ground disturbance, including crop circles.

Close Encounter 3: A UFO encounter in which an entity is present, including humanoids or robots—this is also known as First Contact. The movie, *Close Encounters of the Third*

Kind is based on a true CE 3 experience with Dr. J. Allen Hynek making an appearance in it.

Close Encounter 4: A UFO event in which a human is abducted.

In the 1990s, Dr. Steven Greer added a fifth category:

Close Encounter 5: When a human initiates contact with an extraterrestrial (Dr. Steven Greer's movies *Sirius*, *Unacknowledged*, and *Close Encounters of the Fifth Kind* illustrate this protocol).

Observing Spacecraft and Orbs

There are numerous ways to observe spacecraft and other dimensional beings. Before we talk about those, it is important to actually know how to identify "known" objects in the sky, so you won't be thinking everything is a spacecraft. My focus is on the behavior in the night sky.

Airplanes & Helicopters

Airplanes and helicopters are required to have white anti-collision lights when they are flying at night. They also have a red light on the left wing tip and a green light on the right wing tip. There are strobing white lights on the tips and at the back on larger airplanes as well. You will observe a consistent flashing pattern which will vary between types of airplanes (private, military, or commercial) and helicopters. The brightness will be consistent every time the blink happens in a clear sky. The important thing to notice is the pattern has the same timing between each blink. For example, you may see:

blink...blink...blink...blink

or you may see:

blink blink...blink blink...blink blink...blink blink

If you happen to see blinking lights that are more random in the timing of the pattern or only last for a very short time and then are gone, it is likely not an airplane or helicopter. It may be a spacecraft.

Satellites, Space Station, and Space Junk

Satellites, the International Space Station, and space junk are metallic and do not have blinking lights on them. The sun reflects off the metallic surface, making them visible in the first couple of hours after sunset and a couple of hours before sunrise. They appear as a glowing light traveling in one direction only across the sky at a constant speed. The light will fade as it moves closer to the horizon. The glow does not flicker, blink, or twinkle. The International Space Station is large and close enough that you can see it visibly with your naked eye. It looks like a bright white star with constant, non-blinking, light moving in the sky.

If you watch the movement and glow of a satellite, it is consistent. It will not get brighter and dimmer, and it will not change speed or direction. It will also not disappear in the middle of the sky. Some of the spacecraft can at first appear to be satellites in their movement and consistent glow, but then it does something out of the ordinary. When this happens, it is your cue you have witnessed something "unknown."

Meteorites

Meteorites, also known as shooting stars, are pieces of dust and debris from space that burn up in the Earth's atmosphere. They appear as a bright streak across the sky. To the naked eye, it appears as a fleeting flash of white light with a tail, although up close, it changes from red to white to blue. The flash happens in a fraction of a second. It may emit different colors depending on the mineral content of the debris. When the Earth passes through the dusty trail of a comet or asteroid's orbit, it forms a meteor shower.

Stars and Planets

Stars and planets do not have the movement or the other behavior I just described. They will appear to move very slowly as the Earth is rotating, but there is no obvious movement when you are just looking at them. Stars appear as twinkling lights. Planets appear as a glowing light that doesn't twinkle.

Unknown Activity in the Night Sky

When you are watching the night sky, first notice if the object of interest is blinking or not. If it is blinking in a regular, consistent pattern, it is likely an airplane. If it is not blinking and following a consistent trajectory at a consistent speed, it is likely a satellite. However, if you see odd behavior such as a sudden change in movement or speed, or if there is a noticeable difference in the brightness it is giving off, such as getting really bright and then really dim, it is likely "unknown" and possibly a spacecraft.

On the UFO tours that I lead in Hawaii, we see a lot of unusual behavior when we are looking through the advanced Gen 3 military night vision goggles. For example, we have seen objects first appearing to be satellites but then disappearing in the middle of a sky, perhaps leaving through a portal or shifting to a higher dimension where it is no longer visible. We have seen objects suddenly appear in the middle of the sky as well. We have seen objects that change their brightness in a huge way, going from looking very bright and large in size to very dim and back to bright and so on. Some glowing objects have done sudden movement changes and even zig-zagging motion or looping behavior. Other objects have made very obvious speed changes. Some of the lights we observe have very random patterning and major movement in between the blinks. Some of the behavior I am describing can sometimes be seen with the naked eye.

Orbs and Other Light Objects

Orbs can appear as floating spherical objects of a variety of sizes. They can be visible to the naked eyes. They are often captured by cameras, even when they are not visible to the person taking the picture. Some orbs may be spacecraft. Other orbs are believed to be individual beings from a higher dimension.

I have personally experienced a lot of orbs in different circumstances. In Sedona, several of us on a UFO tour saw a fairly large orange orb while we were waiting for the sky to get dark enough to use the goggles.

When I was at the Ramtha school, we would do different disciplines to communicate with the orbs. One way we did this was by drawing a symbol on an index card (each person would draw their own unique symbol) and meditating as we held it over our heads. The staff would take pictures during the sessions, and the orbs would show shapes inside them which could be linked directly to the index cards. For instance, if someone drew a heart, the orb near the card or next to the person would have a heart inside of it.

Right after I found out I was pregnant with my daughter, a picture was taken of her father and me. In between our heads was a giant blue orb. There were a lot of orbs around me when I was in the hospital about to give birth to her as well.

On one of my UFO tours in Hawaii, one of our guests saw a green orb floating in front of her. There was a mass sighting of a blue orb on the island of Oahu in January of 2021, which was captured on video. It was first in the sky, and then it ended up going into the ocean. As a side note, there is a suspected underwater base off the southern part of Hawaii, and there are a lot of sightings of craft moving in and out of the water.

When viewing the night sky, you may see colored orbs that appear and disappear or move in a direction for a short distance. The color indicates how much energy the ship is using. When the color appears red or orange, it indicates a lower amount of energy, whereas green and blue lights indicate a higher amount of energy.

Other lights and spacecraft have been observed which don't fit any Earth-based craft. The Phoenix Lights incident was a mass sighting in the late 1990s where several lights in the shape of a triangle were observed. Bashar, a hybrid higher dimensional being channeled by Darryl Anka, claims that was his ship.

About 10 years ago, my husband woke up in the middle of the night when he was living in his home in Tacoma, Washington. He looked up through the skylight in his bedroom and saw a rectangular-shaped craft. He and his now ex-wife went outside and watched it for about 10-15 minutes. It was metallic with no visible lights and the size of a football field. It made no noise. After trying to photograph and call their friends with no luck, the ship moved slowly at first and then quickly shot away and disappeared.

My husband, friend, and I saw a large pyramid-shaped craft through the clouds one evening when we were focusing on calling the spacecraft in. The outline was so crisp it was undeniable. I got confirmation later it was the Andromedans.

Occasionally, I see random small lights inside my house that will flash, visible in my peripheral view. The color is either white or blue. These lights are not caused by something explainable. They are higher dimensional beings letting me know they are there.

The more open you are to experiencing interactions with higher dimensional beings, the more likely it will happen. In Chapters 14 and 15, I will teach you different methods to call them in and communicate with them.

In the next chapter, we will begin our exploration of some of the different alien races that have been identified.

SECTION 3: INTRODUCING OUR GALACTIC FRIENDS AND FAMILY

Chapter 9
Alien Races—An Overview

*"I may not know you, but I don't see any difference
between you and me. I see myself in you; we are one."*
— Debasish Mridha

The big question regarding aliens is how many different races exist in our galaxy and in our universe? The answer depends on who you ask. Mainstream science has been searching for the answer but from a limited perspective. In 1960, the Search for Extraterrestrial Intelligence (SETI) was formed by Dr. Frank Drake, an astrophysicist and astronomer from Harvard and Cornell. The purpose of SETI was to use radio telescopes to listen for extraterrestrial transmissions. He came up with what is known as the Drake Equation in 1961. It is used to estimate the number of communicative civilizations (electromagnetic emissions detectable) in the Milky Way Galaxy.

The Drake Equation is as follows: $N = R_* \, f_p \, n_e \, f_l \, f_i \, f_c \, L$

- **N** : The number of civilizations in the Milky Way galaxy whose electromagnetic emissions are detectable.

- **R$_*$** : The rate of formation of stars suitable for the development of intelligent life (number per year).

- f_p : The fraction of those stars with planetary systems.

- n_e : The number of planets, per solar system, with an environment suitable for life.

- f_l : The fraction of suitable planets on which life actually appears.

- f_i : The fraction of life-bearing planets on which intelligent life emerges.

- f_c : The fraction of civilizations that develop a technology that produces detectable signs of their existence.

- L : The average length of time such civilizations produce such signs (years).

If you analyze the equation, Dr. Drake's assumptions of what constitutes intelligent life are really only looking for a planet and environment similar to ours. It assumes life lives above ground rather than inside. It also presumes a technology at the same level as ours, without giving a possibility to more advanced technology which wouldn't be detectable by Earth-based technology at the time.

The Fermi paradox is the conflict between the lack of clear, obvious evidence for extraterrestrial life and various high estimates for their existence. In the 1950s, Fermi stated if there was extraterrestrial life, we should be able to detect them.

As government disclosure is slowly happening and individuals have their own personal undeniable experiences, we know visitation is happening by intelligent lifeforms. Craig

Campobasso identifies 82 different alien races who are known to have interacted with our Earth at some point in his book, *The Extraterrestrial Species Almanac*. Elena Danaan identifies 110 different alien races in her book, *A Gift From the Stars: Extraterrestrial Contacts and Guide of Alien Races*. These numbers are low compared to what some of the channeled extradimensional beings have said through various channels. The Sirius star system alone has been estimated to have at least 10,000 different races.

There are, of course, numerous others (thousands to millions or billions) who have not been documented, including my group from Io. When my friend Lee and I had a session to ask them questions, they said they had very little interaction with Earth and were not part of the Galactic Federation. This explains why they are not known to those in our government and to people like Danaan who claim to interact with the Galactic Federation.

If you happen to read either of the books on alien races I mentioned, I want you to be aware of how the authors describe the beings. Both give a detailed description of where the race is from and whether or not they are considered to be benevolent or malevolent. Danaan's book is more polarized in her presentation of the races, with a fear-based perspective in her writings, in my opinion.

Campobasso's book is less polarized in the way he classifies the races into two major groups. One group believes in the Cosmic Law of One and is of Service to Others. The other group is of Service to Self, which are the species that are generally considered malevolent in Danaan's writings. I don't disagree with either one of them about the existence of polarized alien races who reside in

3rd density. Just look at the range of polarity expressed on Earth. The number of beings existing in the higher dimensions is far greater than those in 3rd density.

In all of the books I've read and channelings I have experienced, in the higher realms of 4th density (5th dimension) and above, there is no polarity. There is no good or bad. There is no right or wrong. We are all from the same source. When we are at this 3rd density level, polarity exists, which helps us to evolve. It's an agent of change for evolution. So even if we experience it as good or bad in our human lives, when seen from a higher perspective, it doesn't have the same judgment factor.

The alien races who are described as being of Service to Self, or malevolent, reside in the 3rd density. As with Earth humans, not all individuals within a race have the same agenda and are at the same level of thinking. Some understand love, while others want to control and manipulate.

Because both of those books give details and illustrations of the alien races within them, I will not duplicate their work. Instead, in this next section, I will give a short overview of some of the races that are connected to Earth. In the following two chapters, I will give more information about the groups who were directly involved in the seeding of Earth from an evolutionary perspective.

The Grays and the "Abduction" Experience

Although there are well over 100 documented alien races, the grays are the most notorious in UFO folklore, receiving the most press since the 1947 Roswell crash. They are thought to be involved in most "abduction" cases.

One question that comes up a lot in the realm of aliens is about alien abductions. Why are they abducting people? What are they doing to them? I want to say in these cases, the person is always returned, so the word abduction is loaded with fear. I love Lyssa Royal Holt's take on this in her channeling. She calls it being temporarily detained, which I have adopted.

There are many species of gray aliens from different star systems, including, but not limited to, Lyra, Orion, Sirius, and Zeta Reticuli. Each gray race has its own agenda ranging from Service to Self to Service to Others. Some of these beings are in polarized 3rd density, and others are in non-polarized 4th density and above.

Although there are accounts regarding several gray races who are involved in temporary detainment, the group most commonly affiliated with the detainment scenarios are known as the Zetas coming from Zeta Reticuli. They are often accompanied by taller grays and Mantis beings who oversee the genetic work being done.

In my research on temporary detainment, some of the people being taken have been done so by the government with staged abductions. There are people who have come forth with this information. Those have tended to be negative experiences.

The people who are taken and experience the real gray aliens have a variety of reactions to the experience. For some, it is a beautiful experience. For others, there is a strong fear reaction, which is likely due to fear of the unknown. From a soul-level incarnation perspective, those involved in any kind of detainment scenario have forgotten at a soul level they agreed to have interaction with the grays (or any other alien race detainment). No one can be taken against their will. This is a hard pill for some to swallow, as they feel victimized and want to stay in that place.

Some of the people who have been aboard craft have been hypnotized to recover their memories. As a past life regression therapist, I understand if they are not taken deep enough into their subconscious mind, they may encounter fear because the ego is still too present. Those who are taken into a much deeper state have the full realization of the larger plan of it all. Dolores Cannon has thousands of examples of this over her many decades of regressing people to a deeper level. Her books highlight some of these cases. My own clients have been able to go deep enough to see their experiences from a higher level and under-standing.

The humans involved in the temporary detainment are part of a hybridization program combining the genetics of the Zetas with Earth humans. Often those detained report their eggs and sperm have been taken from them. Some women know they are pregnant and get confirmation from the doctor, and then the baby is removed from the womb early in development. The doctors are unable to explain why. Some men and women have experienced being able to see their hybrid children. I have a male friend who met 30 of his hybrid children about 10 years ago. I have other friends who know they have hybrid children as well. In Chapter 12, I share the story of the purpose of this hybridization program and who the hybrid races are.

If you are someone who has had this detainment experience, know it is for a greater cause that you agreed to at the soul level before incarnating into this life. If there is unresolved trauma in your life, I encourage you to find practitioners who can help you work through the trauma and to see the bigger picture.

Reptilians and Draconians

The Reptilians and Draconians are other groups who get negative press. The work Dr. Michael Salla has done on gathering research and testimonies from government and military whistleblowing insiders suggests different Reptilian and Draconian groups are directly working on Earth. The Indigenous Reptilians (from Inner Earth) are involved in genetic engineering, elite corruption, and perpetuating religious dogma. The Draconians (from Alpha Draconis) are connected to wealth and poverty, corrupt elites, ethnic and religious violence, terrorism, the drug trade, and organized crime. Several of Dr. Salla's books go into great detail; for quick reference, *Galactic Diplomacy: Getting to Yes With ET* is a place to start.

Some Reptilian and Draconian groups are Service to Self, with other groups being Service to Others. They are not all "negative" in the way they are portrayed. Those in 4th density and above understand love and unity and have evolved beyond polarity.

There are a number of different races coming from several different locations, including, but not limited to, Lyra, Sirius, Orion, Inner Earth, and Draco. Some are cold-blooded (ectothermic) in nature, while others are mammalian with reptile appearance and are warm-blooded (endothermic). Vegans who first came to Earth incorporated reptile DNA into themselves to create a mammalian species with reptilian features. This is one of the groups that has gone inside of the Earth to live.

Mantis

Mantis are bipedal beings who look like praying mantis insects. They are between seven to 10 feet tall with long limbs. They are highly advanced and evolved and are believed to be one of the most ancient groups in the Universe. Some of these beings are referred to as The Founders in the next chapter, as they are said to have created the humanoid form in the galaxy.

Although they reside in 5th density and higher, they have the ability to lower their vibration to 3rd and 4th density in order to have a physical form. They are master geneticists. Some are believed to work with the Zetas on the hybridization program. There are different races coming from Antares, Andromeda, Orion, and beyond. In Danaan's work and Dr. Salla's research, some are considered to be Service to Self and involved in detainment scenarios with the grays. While I agree they work with the Zetas, I don't have the opinion this is a "bad" thing.

Arcturians

Arcturians come from the area of Arcturus in the Bootes constellation. They reside in a higher dimensional, non-physical form, although they have the ability to lower their vibration to interact with Earth humans. They are tall and thin with blue skin and no hair. They have large eyes. They emit an energy of pure love. They are associated with some of the crop circles on Earth. More will be described in Chapter 11 about their relation to Earth.

Lyrans

Lyrans come in a variety of forms and are from the constellation Lyra. They are the original humanoid proto-type which all other humanoid races evolved from. The humanoids originally ranged in skin tone from blue, brown, white, yellow and red. As they evolved over time, their hair, skin, and eyes got lighter. Their relationship to Earth will be covered in Chapter 10.

There are humanoid Lyran groups who have incorporated other animal DNA into the mammalian form, including primate, reptilian, avian, and feline forms.

Vegans

The Vegans are humanoid with darker skin, eyes, and hair, similar to the Native Americans, Aborigines, and Asians. They were the first group to arrive on Earth. They diversified into three main groups: Mammalians, Reptilian Mammalians, and Reptilians. Chapter 10 gives more detail about their relationship to Earth.

Sirians

Sirians come from the Sirius star system. Some are humanoid in form. Others resemble Grays or Reptilians. Sirius is said to have some water planets, giving rise to a variety of aquatic forms. Cetaceans (whales and dolphins) are believed to be from Sirius, as well as other marine life, including sharks, octopus, and merpeople. Life exists in all dimensions in the Sirius system, some physical and others non-physical. There is a strong Earth connection with the Sirians, as will be discussed in more detail in Chapter 10.

Orions

The Orion constellation is home to a number of different races and forms. As with Sirius, some are humanoid, while others are Grays and Reptilians. There are different groups who have interacted with Earth for different reasons. Chapter 10 covers them in detail.

Pleiadians

Pleiadians are humanoid and indistinguishable from Nordic Earth humans. They are from the Pleiades constellation. Their skin is light, but their hair color ranges from light to dark. They are the closest genetically to us. They reside in higher dimensions and interact with Earth, assisting humanity. Chapter 11 gives the history of their connection with Earth.

Cat-like Beings

Cat-like beings are humanoid with feline facial features and tails. They come from Lyra, Sirius, and Antares. They believe in Service to Others. In Egyptian culture, the goddess Bastet is a cat-like deity, perhaps coming from Sirius.

Blue Avians

The Blue Avians come from Lyra and are an avian-mammalian form. They believe in Service to Others and are here to help Earth understand Unity Consciousness.

Andromedans

Andromedans reside in higher dimensions and come from the Andromeda galaxy. Their appearance is blue and hairless, somewhat similar to the Arcturians. They have been described as feeling like heavenly stars—true nirvana. They teach unconditional love and council different star nations. They are associated with some of the crop circles. They focus on peace resolution. Some visit Earth in merkaba-shaped, crystalline-shaped, and diamond/pyramid-shaped craft.

Procyonans

Procyonans come from Procyon and highly resemble Earth Humans. They interact with Earth humans to help elevate their spiritual nature. They are thought to be involved with human rights issues (on the Service to Others spectrum) and may be the possible group helping to expose the secrecy of extraterrestrials, according to Dr. Michael Salla.

Ummites

Ummites come from the planet Ummo from the star Wolf 424. They are indistinguishable from Earth humans. In 1950, Ummite explorers came to Earth to learn about our cultures. They disseminated scientific information about our Universe to specific individuals, including leading scientists, to expand thinking. They provided information on new technology to benefit humanity.

Bigfoot

Bigfoot, also known as sasquatch and yeti, is a bipedal primate connected with Earth. Some authors suggest this group are interdimensional travelers, which is why we have sightings, but no concrete evidence that mainstream science will accept. Author Kewaunee Lapsertitis has two intriguing books on this topic, *The Sasquatch People and Their Interdimensional Connection* and *The Psychic Sasquatch and their UFO Connection*. In the Law of One material channeled by Ra, Bigfoot is said to have originally come from planet Maldek, which was destroyed and is now the asteroid belt between Mars and Jupiter.

Venusians

Venusians come from Venus and live inside the planet. They are indistinguishable from Earth humans. They reside in higher dimensions and have interacted with various Earth humans and the US government.

This is just a small sampling of alien races we know of. In the following two chapters, I will go into much more detail on some of these groups and how they are directly related to the evolution of Earth humans.

Although there are a plethora of humanoid forms throughout the universe, there are even more who look nothing like us. Some humans still have fear and judgment over things that are different from themselves. If we are to have successful contact with other alien races, it is imperative we see the beauty in all forms of life, no matter how weird or bizarre they might first seem.

DIVERSITY EXERCISE: I want you to go out in nature or go online and actively look at different insects or invertebrates. Perhaps look at marine animals, including microscopic ones. Try to find the most bizarre species you can and really look at their form. See the beauty in how different they are from you and from other creatures. Understand how their form is perfect for their environment and lifestyle.

Chapter 10
Galactic Evolution of the Humanoid Form, Part 1

"In this magical life we live, it's as though everyone we've ever met is like a star in the galaxy of our experience and beingness."
— Rasheed Ogunlaru

As a former evolutionary biologist, I have always been fascinated with how life changes over time due to different factors, including environment, habitat, food availability, competition, specialization, interbreeding, and more. Although my specific studies focused on the evolution of fishes, my interest spans all of life.

When I was a graduate student at the University of Chicago in the late 1990s, with my office based at the Field Museum of Natural History, I had ample opportunities to immerse myself in the history of the natural world beyond my study of focus. There was a famous display on human evolution at the museum, with a demonstration of how it was believed humans evolved on Earth. It included the "Lucy" specimen, *Australopithecus afarensis,* thought to be the first human species coming from Africa.

In evolutionary research, there is something known as the "missing link." Missing links are considered obvious transitional species from one group to another. Throughout the animal phylum, we have gaps in different animal species. This includes missing links between various human forms yet to be discovered. There have been significant jumps in the form and function of the human body over time, which cannot be explained by science in our current understanding.

Dr. Arthur Horn, who was a biological anthropologist for many years in mainstream academia (Yale University and Colorado State University), observed that there were too many overlaps between certain human species and very large gaps in how the body was changed between the species. He came up with an Extraterrestrial Intervention Hypothesis, which he explains in his book *Humanity's Extraterrestrial Origins: ET Influences on Humankind's Biological & Cultural Evolution.*

He identifies five major transitions defying explanation and proof in the fossil record:

1. Advanced primates: 40 million years ago (mya)
2. Australopithecines (Hominidae): 4 mya
3. Homo habilis (handy man): 2.5 mya
4. Homo erectus: 1.8 mya
5. Homo sapiens: 300,000 mya

His theories are corroborated by archaeological evidence from cultures around the world put forth by ancient astronaut theorists, as well as with channeled material coming from higher dimensional beings, as will be explained below.

Extraterrestrial Intervention

The concept of aliens coming to Earth and interacting and interbreeding with humans originally came from the translations of tablets from Sumeria in ancient times. The tablets mention the Anunnaki. Although some authors in this field, such as Zecharia Sitchin, denote the Anunnaki as a specific race of beings coming from the planet Nibiru, it more loosely translates as "those from heaven who came to Earth."

When we look at all of the ancient cultures around the world, they share similar stories of otherworldly beings coming from the sky and interacting with humans. These beings are referred to as gods and goddesses. There are some differences in the forms they appear, as in the cultures. In India, you have beings exhibiting blue skin, multiple arms, or snake-like bodies. In Egypt, there are multiple gods and goddesses of various forms, including those with human bodies and various animal heads (dog, bird, feline, etc.). Some are presented as giant humans, such as in Greek mythology.

Each of these different regions and their gods and goddesses has a specific star system they are associated with. For instance, in Hawaii and spanning throughout the Pacific Ocean from Easter Island to Japan and down to New Zealand, they believe the star people come from the Pleiades. People in the Mayan culture, Egypt, and the Dogon tribe in Africa believe they are of Sirian descent.

Ancient artifacts from around the world give credibility to the idea there were highly advanced visitors and/or technology on Earth that could not be produced in some cases, even today. Some of the evidence of these visitors has been destroyed over time through various cataclysms, floods, and the destruction of Atlantis and similar civilizations.

There are varying ideas about how many alien races came to Earth to help evolution along. Alex Collier, an Andromedan contactee, says we have up to 22 different extraterrestrial races that have provided genetic material for humans. Stewart Swerdlow, an experiencer, says we have 13 races that have genetically modified us.

While we may never fully know the exact number of races, we have plenty of evidence that our DNA is different. When the human genome was sequenced, they found places where there were kinks in the strands rather than them being smooth. It appeared exactly as it would if the DNA was genetically modified or spliced in with other DNA. Mainstream science has done its best to explain this anomaly; however, they are simply trying to make a story to fit the scenario because they don't know. This idea of hybrid humans is explored in the book, *Exogenesis: Hybrid Humans: A Scientific History of Extraterrestrial Genetic Manipulation* by Bruce and Daniella Fenton.

There is also the concept of junk DNA, which scientists have long thought to be useless. This makes up 98.5 percent of DNA sequences. Less than two percent of our DNA is believed to be for coding proteins. For those of us who work directly with the extradimensional beings, we know the so-called junk DNA is actually latent DNA that gets activated at certain times in our life when we reach a certain vibratory level. This will be covered more below.

Evolution of the Humanoid Form

Lyssa Royal-Holt is a channel for multiple entities that teach information about various aspects of our relationship with the extraterrestrials and extradimensionals. One particular being who specializes in sharing galactic history is a multidimensional consciousness called Germane. The following information about the galactic evolution was channeled through Lyssa in 1989. I am providing a summary of what Germane shares. For more extensive understanding, please refer to her excellent book, *The Prism of Lyra: An Exploration of Human Galactic Heritage.*

The Founders

The Founders are a group of nonphysical beings who are said to have created the original human form. When they appeared physically, they resembled bipedal insects with large eyes and long limbs. They created an experiment in which they wanted the experience of moving from the whole (unity) to separation with a polarized reality and back to the whole. This would create a polarized reality which could then be integrated. Some of the "offspring" of the Founders played a part in the development of Earth. Other offspring branched off and have not had direct connection or interference with Earth. This section will only focus on those who are directly connected to Earth.

Lyra

The Lyra constellation is the general area where the humanoid race was birthed by the Founders. All humanoid races in our galactic family have genetic roots connected to Lyra. Some of the planets within Lyra began to develop primate life. The Founders seeded the primates with plasmic energy on meta-atomic levels within their DNA. This created groups who were at first the same (homogenous), with no diversity. As time went on, separation and change occurred, where the groups were polarized into positive and negative orientations, with some showing integration.

They evolved and achieved space travel, which helped to expose themselves to other planetary groups. The cultures began to mix. At this point in their development, they had advanced technology, expansive philosophy, and strong social development. The polarities among them split and manifested into other polarities, such that negative polarities split into a group with negative and positive poles. The positive polarities split into positive and negative poles. The experiment was getting out of control with so much fragmentation.

The original Lyrans were humanoid and had a diversity of skin tones ranging from blue, brown, white, yellow and red. As they evolved through time, their skin, hair, and eyes got lighter.

Vega

The first group that branched off from Lyra to become a non-Lyran species were the Vegans. Vega is a star within the constellation of Lyra. They were a polarized group that created a race of beings that manifested Lyra's opposite polarity in belief in actions. When they first branched off, they had negative polarity or service to self. During this

time, there were many conflicts between Lyrans and
Vegans. Some of the Vegan groups left the conflict and
branched out to Altair and Centauri. The Lyrans were also
continuing their expansion into other star systems.

The Vegans tended to be darker-skinned, with darker eyes
and hair, similar to the Native Americans, Aborigines, and
Asians. In their temperament, they are likened to the
Vulcans from Star Trek, with high telepathy, spiritual
connection, and physical strength.

The Vegans were the first humanoid group to travel to
Earth during the early part of the dinosaur era, claiming it
as their own. Some of them mixed in reptilian DNA into
their own, which ultimately created three separate species:
1) Mammalian Vegan, 2) Reptilian Vegan, and 3)
Reptilian. Some of these Reptilian Vegans migrated to
Orion and back to Lyra.

Some original Vegans also moved to Sirius and Orion.
Those who went to Orion reclaimed esoteric knowledge
from the Founders and went deeper into their spirituality to
begin the path of Vegan mysticism. This is the root of
several spiritual lineages on Earth, including Tibetan
culture prior to Buddhism, Vedic culture before Hinduism,
and the spiritual cultures of Native Americans in America
and Mexico. These ideas were brought to Earth at a later
time.

A group of Lyrans came to Earth at the end of the dinosaur
era, causing conflict between the established Earth Vegans
and the newly arrived Lyrans. Some of the Vegans left
Earth, as mentioned above, and some went underground,
inside the Earth.

Sirius

After colonizing Vega, Sirius was one of the first areas to be colonized by Lyrans. Sirius is a trinary star group (Sirius A, B and C), which became an important symbol for the entire galactic family. Sirius attracted many consciousnesses who chose to remain nonphysical, creating a large variety of consciousness types. A group of Sirians transmuted their energy into matter, creating a 3rd density world that could support physical life.

Some of the Sirians became the earliest genetic and etheric engineers, following in the footsteps of the Founders. They created realms for all different manifestations of consciousness and became known as the Elders of Sirius.

Vegans who were highly polarized in the masculine moved into the 3rd density reality of Sirius. They had a philosophy of domination, and they lost their memory connection to Vega. A nonphysical group from Lyra that was polarized toward the idea of Service to Others moved into Sirius. They were interested in healing those in physical pain. The Lyran positive group sent love and healing energy to the masculine group, which created friction. The Elders of Sirius relocated this conflict away from Sirius to the area of Orion.

Sirians came to Earth to share their knowledge and enhance the physical body of Earth humans. They are connected to ancient Egypt, the Mayan culture, and the Dogon tribe in Africa. In Egypt, they densified their frequency to become visible to 3rd density humans and appeared as the gods and goddesses, including Isis, Osiris, and Anubis. They gave Egyptians, and other cultures advanced astronomical and medical information.

The Mayans were incarnated directly from Sirius to experience physicality. The Sirians shared with them the technology of transmutation, of changing from matter to pure energy and consciousness, which is how they appeared to suddenly disappear from Earth as a group. The Sirians left behind many puzzles of their interactions, including the crystal skulls found in the Mayan region of the world.

Many early Sirians were adept at genetic engineering. During the Earth Inception, the Sirians placed a latent DNA code within early humans. When Earth reaches a certain vibratory frequency as a race, the code will be triggered, assisting remembrance of our galactic past. Genetic engineering by the Sirians was also used to upgrade the physical human body to be able to hold more energy of a higher frequency. As I've shared, I have memories of being one of these Sirian genetic scientists.

Although the polarized conflict was moved away from Sirius to Orion, other polarized groups migrated to Sirius. The practice of black magic and the dark arts is rooted in the philosophy of the negative Sirians. In Egypt, this practice took place in the temples of Set. This has also manifested the group known as the Illuminati. They are a group of physical and nonphysical negatively oriented extraterrestrials who came to Earth during the Inception. They have an agenda of control. However, they can only be an influence if one allows them. We were given free will on Earth, and we have the power over ourselves.

Other negative Sirian influences on Earth include cattle mutilations, the "Men in Black" phenomenon, and negative UFO experiences. They want to keep Earth from shifting to 4th density, as they fear they will no longer exist. Sirius is ultimately a triad and represents the integration of polarity. This is the destiny of Earth.

Positive Sirians help with the physical healing of Earth humans. It is the most widely used energy on Earth. The positive Sirians (physical healers) who remained in the Sirius area allied themselves with Arcturus, which has the energy of emotional healing. Together they form the Sirius/Arcturus Matrix, which is the healing of mind, body, and spirit.

Orion

The conflict that arose in Sirius was moved to the Orion constellation, seeding from Sirius, Lyra, and Vega. It became the main battleground for the integration of polarity. The negative side perpetuated Service to Self, which led to domination, genetic manipulation of bloodlines and black magic. The positive side was about Service to Others, even at the expense of themselves.

The Orions evolved into a state of technological advancement while still being in intense spiritual conflict. The book and movie series, *Star Wars*, is the memory of this conflict brought forth to our awareness. This was a time in history known as the Orion Wars, which had conflict playing out between the "Empire" and "The Black League" (the Jedi).

Some positive Orions were able to escape from the Orion Matrix and incarnated on Earth, entering Earth's reincarnation cycle. They were unconsciously playing out the Orion drama in their soul pattern. Some of the negative Orions also entered the Earth cycle, bringing with them the desire for control. The Fall of Atlantis, the Roman Empire, the Nazis, and ongoing religious wars are examples of memory patterns from Orion, which are here on Earth to be cleared.

Negative Orion experiences on Earth currently are with the "Men in Black" and the "Illuminati" (as from Sirius).

At some point in the Orion history, after generations of conflict, a soul incarnated, known as the Orion Christ. He helped them to integrate positivity and negativity to the balance point, demonstrating one must love, not fear. Contemporary Orion has healed its conflict.

Integrated Orions moved outward in the galaxy for a fresh start. Some came to Earth where free will/choice was the primary tool. They were also aware of the latent DNA code that would trigger a desire for societal preservation when and if it became possible for them to self-destruct.

In the next chapter, we will continue the story of the influence of aliens on Earth.

Chapter 11
Galactic Evolution of the Humanoid Form, Part 2

"Moon dust in your lungs; stars in your eyes. You are a child of the cosmos and ruler of the skies."
— Medusa

We continue the story of Galactic interaction and influence on Earth.

Pleiades

The Pleiades constellation was colonized first by Lyran offshoots, who initially went to Earth before moving to the Pleiades. A group of Lyrans went to Earth and became an Earth-Lyran race, colonizing the area of Scandinavia. They incorporated primate genetics into themselves to assimilate better to Earth's environment. A different group of Lyrans was on Earth at the same time and were inserting Lyran genetics into primates, creating a conflict.

The Earth-Lyrans left Earth to go to the Pleiades, where they wanted to create a culture based on harmony, truth, and unconditional love. They were living the intuitive feminine polarity. Other Lyrans began to colonize the Pleiades, attracted by the desire to create a community lifestyle. They evolved at a healthy rate, balancing their philosophical/spiritual nature with technology and were stable for thousands of years.

At some point, they became stagnant in their evolution, as there was no conflict in their lives. Some of them joined the Orion struggle, fighting against the negative forces. Others were asked by the Lyrans to return to Earth due to their terrestrial DNA, becoming the main genetic connection from non-Earth sources for humans.

The Pleiadians were directly involved with the development of the Earth human species. They spent thousands of years interacting with most of the primitive cultures on Earth. Ancient documents, drawings, and carvings on cave walls and rocks record this interaction of the "gods." They played a huge role in Lemuria and the islands and countries of the Pacific Ocean.

Although the contact with the Pleiadians has slowed down in modern times compared to the past, they are here to assist humanity. They are the most similar to Earth humans physically and are generally depicted as Nordic looking.

Apex to Zeta Reticuli

A third civilization formed from Lyra, which was a mixture of the Lyra and Vega polarities. This was called the Apex planet. The diversity was even greater than currently on Earth. They could not resolve the polarity, which led to a nuclear war. The devastation of the nuclear blast propelled the Apex planet into an alternate dimension. The survivors of the explosion went underground.

When the Apex planet shifted dimensions after the nuclear explosion, it moved to the Zeta Reticuli system. The survivors who had gone underground only realized the shift had occurred after many generations of being underground when they finally emerged onto the surface. Their bodies had changed so much that they were now a new species, the Zetas.

Zetas were mentally and intellectually highly developed, with large cranium size. The large heads made natural childbirth impossible. They became sterile over several generations, which led to cloning being the mechanism of reproduction. Their bodies became small through genetic engineering. They became a group mind. The lack of sunlight led to their eyes becoming larger and the pupil covering the entire eye to take in more light. The lack of fresh food led them to adapt by getting their nourishment from absorbing frequencies of light. Their organs atrophied from non-use. Their skin became photovoltaic (converting light to electrical energy) and photothermic (converting light to heat).

Some of the more negatively-oriented individuals left the former Apex planet and went to areas of Sirius and Orion (Betelgeuse, specifically). Others went to a different planet in the Zeta Reticulum system. The neutral and positively-oriented Zetas reestablished connection with the Founders.

From all the cloning, the Zetas had bred emotions out of their race, and they became stagnant in their evolutionary growth. Beginning in the 1940s, they became intimately connected with Earth, as they desired to breed back in a mixture of other human species. Earth humans had the mixture desired, including the characteristics of physiological and neurological emotions. They are the primary group instigating "temporary detainments." By combining the Zeta and Earth human DNA, they are creating a new advanced hybrid race. This race is the ultimate integration the Founders desired at the beginning of their experiment.

Hybrids

Hybrid, as defined here, refers to the combining of Zeta and Earth human DNA. This is a soul contract before the human is born on Earth. Most people forget they volunteered to help and agreed to the contract, which is why fear happens. The intent of hybridization is to face the shadow, the opposite of self and to love it, embrace it, and become it. It is to be both unified and diverse, filled with unconditional love.

There are two major groups of hybrids with subcategories for each. One group is the Essassani, which are half Zeta and half Earth human who live on ships. They may be the first ones to integrate with us by living here on Earth. The other group is the Yahyel, which are Zetas and Earth humans who are very human-like.

Arcturus

The Arcturus involvement with Earth is different from the other groups we have talked about so far. The Arcturians and the Founders worked hand-in-hand with the humanoid experiment. Arcturus is a higher dimensional reality that acts as a dimensional gateway to Earth. All those who incarnate on Earth pass through the Arcturian realm before reaching the planet, which provides healing to those born. There are some who consciously choose not to move through the Arcturus gateway. Likewise, at death, human consciousness passes through the Arcturian realm. It is the perceived light at the end of the tunnel and in near-death experiences.

Arcturus is an archetype of an ideal Earth. The Arcturians primarily exist in 6th density and have been attributed to the angelic kingdom. They are also perceived as a Christ or Buddha frequency. They manifest to Earth humans according to the belief of the person experiencing them. For instance, if a person is religious or believes in angels, they will appear as angels. For people like me, they appear more like aliens. For others, they show up as our future selves. All of this is correct. No matter how the manifestation shows up, they embody love. They are felt as an energy of unconditional love and a surge of creativity.

Arcturians are here to be of service to denser realities, such as Earth. They aid in the consciousness from many levels of awareness. In addition to Earth, they serve physicality and interact with other worlds whose evolution is different from humanoids, including plants, minerals, and animals. Their primary service for physical beings is that of emotional healing.

Arcturians have no karmic debt, so rather than incarnating on Earth into a physical body through birth, they instead "walk in" to an existing body. If there is a soul of a human who is in emotional pain, the human soul will enter the Arcturus realm for healing, and the Arcturian will temporarily inhabit the Earth body. The Arcturus vibration heals, nurtures, and rejuvenates the human spirit.

The Arcturian energy is infused with creativity. When one is creating, their energy aligns with the Creator. It is the vibration of creation, healing, and evolution. The reminder to humanity of the unseen connection to Source and the Arcturian emotional healing energy is triggered by the presence of lenticular clouds. They are associated with some of the crop circles on Earth as well.

Although they primarily reside in 6th density, some of them have densified themselves enough to be perceived by humans. When they are observed in physical form, they are blue-skinned, hairless, with tall thin bodies and enlarged eyes. They interacted with the early culture of Lemuria by teaching healing skills. This was before the Pleiadian influence. When other groups started infiltrating Lemuria, the Earth-based Arcturians went underground to become caretakers of the planet's energy. Although the statues of Easter Island are thought to be connected to the Pleiadians, Germane (the multidimensional being who Lyssa Royal-Holt channels) says they actually pay tribute to Arcturian teachers of Lemuria.

In order to connect with the Arcturian energy, one has to look inward to experience them rather than outward. Working with the combination of the Arcturus/Sirius Matrix, Earth humans have the ability to heal mind, body, and spirit.

Inner Earth

When we talked about the Vegans who had incorporated reptilian DNA into themselves, there was a subset of the group who went inside of Earth, known as Inner Earth.

When the fighting started in Lemuria with other star
groups, the Earth-based Arcturians went inside as well to
maintain the planetary energy. As time progressed in
Lemuria and the continent was on the brink of collapse, a
group of Lemurians went to Inner Earth. A group of
humans from Atlantis, the positive priests, went underground before the destruction. The Lemurian and Atlantis
groups created a dynamic civilization within the Earth, and
they are collectively referred to as the Agarthans. The
beings exist now in a 4th and 5th density reality.

There are underground tunnels throughout the Earth that
the Inner Earth beings move through. The capital city is
called Telos and resides under Mt. Shasta. Another major
city is called Catharia, which sits beneath the Aegean Sea.
Ka Aree is one of the high priestesses of Inner Earth. Saint
Germaine is an Ascended Master who resides in Telos.

Lemuria and Atlantis

For those not aware of the history of Lemuria or Atlantis,
the full history of those continents is beyond the scope of
this book. To summarize, Lemuria was a large continent in
the Pacific Ocean that spanned from Easter Island to
Hawaii and through Polynesia, Indonesia, and Micronesia
down to the islands of New Zealand. It existed culturally
before the time of Atlantis and continued as a
contemporary of Atlantis. Lemuria slowly sank into the
ocean, and the islands of those countries I mentioned are
the mountain remnants of the continent. The Lemurian
culture was spiritually advanced. It was initially influenced
by the Arcturians and then taken over by the Pleiadians.

The Pleiadian stories remain in the current cultures of those countries.

Atlantis was located in the area of the Atlantic Ocean. As a culture, it formed well after Lemuria was already established. It was much more technologically advanced than spiritually advanced, which is what ultimately led to its downfall. It had the influence of the Sirians and the Orions. Remnants of the Atlantis culture were continued in the Sumerian and ancient Egyptian cultures.

As you consider the information about our galactic evolution and the seeding of Earth, take what resonates with you and leave the rest. History is told from a certain perspective. The history I have shared with you comes from a higher dimensional being with no specific polarized agenda. In the work I have done in this realm and experiences I have had to remember who I am, as well as the work I have done with clients, this history sits in truth for me.

Remembering my Arcturian roots and understanding the connection of Arcturus with Lemuria and Inner Earth have put together pieces of the puzzle of my timelines. One of my Arcturian sisters has had vivid memories of the conflict in Lemuria when other star groups, such as the Lyrans, were infiltrating the continent. We didn't understand the history at the time of her regression and dreams, but it makes much more sense now in light of the channeled information from Germane.

My connection to Egypt and the Mayan culture resonates as well. I never felt like I had had a specific Earth-based life in Egypt and wasn't quite sure of the connection to the Mayans. For some reason, I knew they were both important parts of my existence. Now I remember the seeding and genetic modification and being part of that process from the perspective of the Sirians.

In the next chapter, I guide you on a meditative journey to meet your galactic family and guides.

CULTURAL EXERCISE: Think about the areas and history of the cultures of the world for which you have a strong affinity (you may or may not understand why). Perhaps it could be linked to your parallel lives of living among them and interacting with the different star visitors. Make a list of these areas and their associated star people. Notice any emerging patterns.

Chapter 12
Journey to Meet Your Galactic Family & Guides

"You hold the universe in you. You hold the galaxies."
— Twinkle Sharma

If we want to take this journey of connecting with other life forms, then the first thing we have to do is connect with ourselves. We have to know ourselves, learn to love ourselves, and from that point, contact is possible. Otherwise, our contact experiences are not pure—often, we just end up contacting our own inner demons. Then from that experience, we label the other lifeforms as hostile. It always comes back to the self. That is where our evolution is leading. We have to make a connection with each other and ourselves if we want to make a connection with the stars.

I recommend you record this meditation and play it back for yourself, so you can fully relax and take the journey. You can play it back as many times as needed to understand your connection to your family. Let the images flow to you easily and without judgment. Even if you think you are making it up, go with it. Let yourself have the experience. You cannot create something in your mind which does not already exist. Prepare yourself for the journey by getting yourself into a comfortable position, sitting or lying down.

Journey to Meet Your Galactic Family and Guides

Go ahead and close your eyes and start taking some nice deep long breaths. Adjust your body so that you are comfortable and relaxed. Take a deep breath in and hold, then release, letting out all of the air. Take another deep breath in and hold; as you breathe out, your muscles relax. Tension is leaving the body. Continue to breathe, and as you do, your body becomes more and more relaxed. You are safe. All is well.

In your mind's eye, imagine a beautiful stream of white sparkling light above your head, like a waterfall. Open up the top of your head, your crown chakra, to let the shimmering white light flow into your head and make its way through your body, down behind your eyes, into your neck and shoulders, down into your arms, your chest, moving now through your hip area, into your legs and then out through your feet and into the ground. Continue imagining this stream of white light, like a waterfall, a river moving through you. As it moves through you, it relaxes every part of your body. It is removing any blocks or tension you may be holding on to. Allow it to move freely from the top of your head, down through your body and out the bottom of your feet into the ground.

Each breath you take gets you deeper and deeper into your subconscious mind, more and more relaxed. The white shimmering light pours into the top of your head, cleansing away the debris, the cobwebs. Every sound takes you deeper and deeper. All is well. All is well. You are going to go on a journey to meet your galactic family, your galactic guides. Allow yourself to have this experience. You are connected with the universe. You are one with the universe.

As you are relaxed, imagine every cell in your body vibrating. Notice how each of the cells is vibrating together with the other ones around it. All of your cells are in harmony with each other. As you are watching this vibration, the frequency begins to increase, and the vibration is getting faster. Your individual cells are starting to get fainter as the vibration increases. Your body is lighter as your vibration gets higher and higher.

Now we are going to align your chakras with the colors. Start at the base of your spine, which is red. See the red energy. Now focus three inches below your navel with the color orange. Now focus on the solar plexus with the color yellow. Move to your heart and focus on the color green. Now move to your throat and focus on the color blue. Move to your third eye, imagining the color indigo. Focus on your crown with the color violet. Now imagine that your crown opens, and the energy from the heavens comes in through your crown, filling your entire body, as you did earlier. Imagine your root chakra at the base of your spine opens, and the energy of the earth comes through that chakra and fills your body. These two energies—the earth and the sky—meet and entwine your heart. It is from this heart energy, which is a combination of the sky and the earth that you allow yourself to remember that you are part of a greater family, a galactic family. Let that knowledge give you a sense of security and joy. You are not alone.

In front of you, imagine a shimmering tunnel, like a water slide. The colors of the tunnel glisten from green to blue to

117

purple. On the other side of the tunnel is a new time and place, somewhere beyond this Earth. The tunnel calls to you to enter it, enticing you to take the slide to the other side. You are safe. This tunnel will protect you like a warm blanket.

Prepare yourself to enter the tunnel. You may wish to sit down or lay down while riding the tunnel. You may wish to jump into it. Whatever you choose, prepare yourself. Ready, set, go—now you are in this beautiful tunnel of time and space, sliding easily through the tunnel.

As you near the end of the tunnel, you see a glowing white light. Within that light is your galactic family, your galactic guides. Your tunnel ride is now over, and you are surrounded by the glowing white light. You feel a presence within the light, something so familiar, so loving. You are not afraid because you know this is your family or your guides who are always there for you. It's like no time separation has occurred. As your eyes get adjusted to the light, shapes start to take place in front of you. The white light fades away, giving you the ability to see who is in front of you.

Notice the details of the being or beings there with you. Don't judge what you are seeing. There is no right or wrong. If you are unable to see anything, feel the presence and imagine what they might look like. Make it up if you have to.

What impressions are coming to you? What do they look like? How tall are they? What are they wearing, if anything? Do they have hair? If so, what does it look like? What color are their eyes? Look at their hands. What do they look like? If they have fingers, how many do they have? Feel the love of these beings. They are so happy to have you with them.

They have a message for you. This message may come as a feeling. It might come into your head through telepathic thought. It might be heard through your ears or come through a touch. Take a moment to get the message your galactic family has for you.

Look into the eyes of your family, seeing into their soul. Let them see you. Really feel into those eyes. As you are looking into their eyes, receive the love from them.

Now take their hands into yours. Feel the energy exchange between you and your family. Your cells are vibrating at a high frequency. You can feel the buzzing and tingling of your body. As your vibration increases, your physical body starts to become transparent. You are beginning to merge with this being until you are one and the same. You and the being are now one. All of the love they gave you is now inside of you, a part of you forever. You are the love. You are one. There is no separation, only unity.

This love is shining like a bright green light emanating from your heart. Take notice of this shimmering green light beaming out from your heart. Feel the sensation of the light energy expanding beyond your body. Push the light out farther and farther, expanding it beyond space as far as you can. Feel the vibration, the energy, of the green light that is beaming from your heart. You are the source of the light, which is pure love. You are creating the light. It comes from within you. This is who you really are.

Take a moment to really feel the energy of the green light within you. This pulsating beautiful green light.

Say to yourself, "I am love." I am love. I am love. Feel the love. Be the love.

Go ahead and bring the green light back fully into your body, into your heart chakra, still beaming bright. This green light is part of your essence. It is pure love. It is you.

Coming from this place of love, knowing you are one with your galactic family, you have a direct connection any time you want or need it. You have a direct connection to the universe. Everything is connected; there is no separation. Take a moment to ask your galactic family to show you signs they are there with you. This might be a particular ship sighting. It might be in the form of an object or a saying that you might hear or see. It might come to you in a dream. Ask them to come to you, to show themselves to you in the Earth plane, if it is safe for them to do so. Take a moment to thank your galactic family for being there with you.

Counting backward from five to one, you will begin to come back to the current time and place. Five, you are bringing back the full awareness of your self-love and the unity of connection with your galactic family. You know you can call on them when you need them. Four, you are the beautiful green light of love. It is not separate from you. There is no separation in the higher realms of the universe. Three, you are coming back, becoming aware of your consciousness, remembering the message that your galactic family shared with you, knowing they will give you signs they are with you. Two, you are coming back closer and closer, starting to wiggle your fingers and toes. One, you are back to your body. You can slowly open your eyes in your own time.

Remember who and what you are. You are love. You are one with your galactic family. You are one with the Universe. Thank you so much for taking the time to go on this beautiful journey with me.

JOURNAL EXERCISE:

Describe in detail what you saw and how you felt:

What was the message you received?

What was the gift you received?

SECTION 4: CONNECTING TO AND RECEIVING GUIDANCE FROM THE ALIENS

Chapter 13
Benefits and Signs of Connections to the Aliens

"When the universe wants to communicate, it sends a
dream. If the dreamer is awake, it sends a bird."
— Michael Bassey Johnson, Song of a Nature Lover

In this chapter, we will talk about the benefits of working with the aliens. You will learn some of the signs you are being contacted or are connected with them energetically. At the end is a meditative journey to activate your DNA for a stronger connection to your galactic family.

The Benefits of Working With Aliens

There are so many benefits of working with alien energy. When you really start to understand who and what aliens are and why they are here, it releases any fear you have about them or even about death and the afterlife. The more you work with them, the easier it is to remember who you are and where you came from. You are not just this one Earth life. You are multiple parallel lives in places and dimensions. You are part of Source, the Universe, God, whatever it is you choose to call it, expressing yourself as an individual.

The aliens are our space family, and we can learn much from them about love and healing. It allows you to see your Earth life from a higher perspective and realize we are all connected. It helps to give you a sense of purpose in this Universe. It gets you out of your polarity and judgment of other people. You increase your capacity to come from a place of love, which increases the quality of your relationships with people.

We are all connected. We are one. We have the ability to create our reality. We are not alone. The truth is inside of us.

Signs of Connection to Aliens

You may already experience different signs you are being contacted or have some connection with aliens. The following are some of the signs you may be receiving.

Do you ever have a ringing in one of your ears that isn't tinnitus? I have this all the time. I learned as a teenager from Ramtha that this experience is the aliens trying to send you a message, but because the frequency is so high, we can't interpret the message. Other people have indicated the ringing could be part of activating your DNA or upgrading the body. When this happens, I notice it and acknowledge their transmission in my mind. I notice any other sensations in my body. I thank them for being there with me.

Other people experience music in their ears. This actually happened to me recently when I was woken up by loud music at about two in the morning. I was staying at a hotel with my best friend, leading my Sacred Soul Kona Retreat.

I got out of bed to find out where the music was coming from, looking out on the lanai towards town. There was no sound anywhere externally. It was all in my head. My friend, who is a very light sleeper, did not wake up at all. I realized it was just for me. That night I had a continuous stream of music and toning alternating in my head. Earlier in the evening, we had done our night sky watch and galactic connection exercise, so looking back, I know it was related.

Some experience seeing Light Language symbols when their eyes are closed. These symbols resemble hiero-glyphics. They carry an energy with a message, but not necessarily a direct translation.

Some people, including myself, experience seeing beings with their eyes closed in meditation and in a dream state. This is how I first met my Arcturian family. I continue to have connections with a lot of different beings this way.

One sign of my Mantis group being around has shown up in the form of actual mantis insects being in my space. This has happened a few times in the last few months and was not a coincidence.

Do you see sparkles of light or flashes of light near you? Generally, I will see flashes out of the corner of my eyes at random times. These lights are usually white or blue. They are higher dimensional beings in your space.

Another way to connect is to call them in and then take photos. Orbs, plasma, or other phenomena may show up in your photos. This is something I used to do consistently. If I was taking a picture where I didn't want them to be there, such as in my interior design photos, I would ask them to move out of the way. They would oblige.

Some people see actual craft appear in front of them or up in the sky. If they show themselves to you in this way, it is meant for you to see. Because of my regular connection and appreciation for them, they show up for me when I go to look for them on our UFO tours or randomly out in my yard.

The signs are all around you, and your senses are picking them up, whether or not you are aware of them. When you start paying attention, the more you will experience and deepen the connection you have with your galactic family and guides.

DNA Activation Meditation For Stronger Connectivity

This is a meditative journey to raise your vibration, activate your DNA for a stronger connection to other dimensions, and vector in your location. If we want to take a journey of connecting with other life forms, then the first thing we have to do is connect with ourselves and raise our vibration. We have to know ourselves, learn to love our-selves, and from that point, contact is possible. It always comes back to the self. That is where our evolution is leading. We have to make a connection with each other and ourselves if we want to make a connection with the stars.

I want you to be able to give yourself permission to take this journey. I recommend recording this for yourself and replaying it to take the actual journey.

Get yourself into a nice, comfortable position. Go ahead and close your eyes and start taking some nice deep long breaths. Adjust your body so that you are comfortable and relaxed. Take a deep breath in and hold, then release, letting out all of the air.

Take another deep breath in and hold. As you breathe out, your muscles relax. Tension is leaving the body. Continue to breathe, and as you do, your body becomes more and more relaxed. You are safe. All is well.

In your mind's eye, imagine a beautiful stream of white sparkling light above your head, like a waterfall. Open up the top of your head, your crown chakra, to let the shimmering white light flow into your head and make its way through your body, down behind your eyes, into your neck and shoulders, down into your arms, your chest, moving now through your hip area, into your legs and then out through your feet and into the ground.

Continue imagining this stream of white light, like a waterfall, a river moving through you. As it moves through you, it relaxes every part of your body. It is removing any blocks or tension you may be holding on to. Allow it to move freely from the top of your head and down through your body and out of the bottom of your feet into the ground.

Each breath you take gets you deeper and deeper into your subconscious mind, more and more relaxed. The white shimmering light pours into the top of your head, cleansing away the debris, the cobwebs. Every sound takes you deeper and deeper. All is well. All is well.

Now we are going to align your chakras with the colors. Start at the base of your spine, which is red. See the red energy. Now focus three inches below your navel with the color orange. Now focus on the solar plexus with the color yellow. Move to your heart and focus on the color green. Now move to your throat and focus on the color blue. Move to your third eye, imagining the color indigo. Focus on your crown with the color violet.

Now imagine your crown opens, and the energy from the heavens comes in through your crown, filling your entire body, as you did earlier. Imagine your root chakra at the base of your spine opens, and the energy of the earth comes through that chakra and fills your body. These two energies—the earth and the sky—meet and entwine your heart. It is from this heart energy, which is a combination of the sky and the earth that you allow yourself to remember that you are part of a greater family, a galactic family. Let this knowledge give you a sense of security and joy. You are not alone.

As you are relaxed, imagine every cell in your body vibrating. Notice how each of the cells is vibrating together with the other ones around it. All of your cells are in harmony with each other. As you are watching this vibration, the frequency begins to increase, and the vibration is getting faster. Your individual cells are starting to get fainter as the vibration increases. Your body is lighter as your vibration gets higher and higher.

Go inside one of your cells. Inside the cell is the nucleus, which holds your DNA. Visualize the double helix of the DNA within this cell. Scan the DNA from above. Intuitively go to the part of the DNA that is ready to be activated today, which will allow you to connect to higher dimensions more easily.

Imagine that part of the DNA helix splitting apart. As it is split apart, imagine a burst of white light energy moving through the split helix. This white light energy activates this part of the DNA to replicate itself, which then activates something new and fantastic inside of you. When you come out of this journey, you will know you have a new activation that will make your connection to your galactic family stronger. It allows you to raise your vibration easier, to release the density of 3D earth.

Allow the double helix to form back together and pull yourself out of the nucleus and then out of the cell. See the cell, glowing gold, vibrating at a very high rate, where it is almost invisible. You can see the glowing energy, but you can't quite make out the exact structure of the cell. Now pull yourself back even farther to see every cell in your body vibrating at a very high frequency, glowing gold.

Now, take note of your heart chakra. See the green glowing light emanating from your heart space. Feel the sensation of the green light energy expanding beyond your body. Push the light out farther and farther, expanding it beyond space as far as you can. Feel the vibration, the energy, of the green light that is beaming from your heart. You are the source of the light, which is pure love. You are creating the light. It comes from within you. This is who you really are.

Take a moment to really feel the energy of the green light within you. This pulsating beautiful green light. Say to yourself, "I am love." I am love. I am love. Feel the love. Be the love.

Go ahead and bring the green light back fully into your body, into your heart chakra, still beaming bright. This green light is part of your essence. It is pure love. It is you.

Coming from this place of love, you have a direct connection to the universe. Use your mind and your connection to identify where your galactic family is located. Imagine from their perspective of looking down on Earth. Now slowly zoom in to your country, closer to your state, now to your city, to your neighborhood, and your exact house. You are vectoring them in on exactly where to find you, to connect with you. Welcome them in. There is no fear, only love.

Counting backward from five to one, you will begin to come back to the current time and place. Five, you are bringing back the full awareness of your self-love and the unity of connection with the universe. Four, you are the beautiful green light of love. It is not separate from you. There is no separation in the higher realms of the universe. Three, you are coming back, becoming aware of your consciousness, knowing that you have activated your DNA for easier connection and communication. You know how to raise your vibration and to call them to you. Two, you are coming back closer and closer, starting to wiggle your fingers and toes. Remember who and what you are. You are love. You are one with the Universe. One, you are back to your body. You can slowly open your eyes in your own time.

In the next chapter, we will explore different modalities of ways to connect and receive guidance.

Chapter 14
Ways to Connect and Receive Guidance, Part 1

"The dancing Sun, the dancing moon, the dancing stars and the dancing galaxies are the direct expression of our divine Self."
— Amit Ray

There are numerous ways to connect and receive guidance from beyond our 3rd density reality. In this chapter, we will cover different practices you can do to enhance your ability to connect. What I want to remind you is that most connections and guidance are received when we are in a relaxed state of mind.

There are some people who dismiss the inner connection because they want to have physical, tangible proof of alien life. What I will say is that it is all a real connection and deeper than the physical level. Science doesn't have the tools to measure this, but that does not make it false. Going inward and connecting is the way to do it. All dreams, daydreams, and experiences are real, including those in drug-induced states.

The more you are able to raise your vibration, let go of judgment of yourself and everyone around you, and come from a place of love, the more you will experience extradimensional beings. This includes the fairies, Ascended Masters, angels, and aliens. They all reside in higher densities and higher dimensions. You have the ability to raise your frequency. The more you practice this, the closer you are to living in a 5th dimensional world where instant manifestation happens and polarity doesn't exist. What a beautiful world this will be.

The Clairs

You do not need to be psychic to connect with higher dimensional beings. All humans have built-in intuition and abilities beyond the five senses we experience in our waking life. Some people have developed certain senses to be more in tune. Anyone can enhance their *clairs* with practice and trust.

What are the clairs? They are types of psychic connection, tuning into extra-sensory perception. There are several clairs described below.

Clairvoyance: Clear seeing; seeing images in your mind. Notice any random images which pop into your mind. These may be clairvoyant messages.

Clairaudience: Clear hearing; hearing messages, music, or tones in your head. Notice hearing your name when no one is calling it or other words or sounds in your head that is not coming from an outside source or from your ego-mind. These may be clairaudient messages.

Clairsentience: Clear feeling; sensing the emotions and feelings around you; you may feel it in your body. Notice any random feelings or emotions coming to you that don't have a direct relation to what you personally are experiencing. This can also come as a gut feeling or chills in your body.

Claircognizance: Clear knowing; knowing something without needing proof. Notice things you just know to be true without needing to compile proof or validation. A thought may randomly come to you.

Clairalience: Clear smelling; smelling things at a heightened level or things not physically present. Notice any smells which come to you that have no physical counterpart in your environment, such as a floral or cigarette smell. You may also be able to "smell" that something is not right.

Clairgustance: Clear tasting; tasting something that isn't actually there or a heightened sense of taste. Notice if you taste something in your mouth that isn't present. You may also be able to taste the details of things others cannot. You may be able to "taste" that something is off.

You may realize you already have one or more of these developed, and you didn't recognize it. You do not need to have all of them to have a connection. Just start paying attention to what is coming to you in these various forms. You are intuitive. You are connected. Trust it.

Meditation

Meditation is not a one size fits all activity. It can be done in many ways, so there really isn't a right or wrong way to do it. From my experience, all of the meditation practices and styles I have learned over the years have one thing in common. They allow you to come back to yourself. Some styles are meant to focus your mind, while others are meant to relax and free your mind from thoughts. Meditation can last as little as seconds up to hours. It all depends on what style appeals to you and what you are trying to achieve. Here are some different techniques for you to try. Most of these can be done sitting or lying down.

1. Focus only on your breathing. This brings you to the present time in your body.

2. Visualize a symbol, image or words in your head, holding the image for as long as possible. This helps in manifestation.

3. Empty your mind, releasing all thoughts. This allows you to shut your mind down to experience the void. It also allows wisdom from the higher self and higher dimensional beings to communicate.

4. Take a self-led journey or follow the words of someone leading you on a journey. This focuses your mind on visuals.

5. Run white light through your body from your crown chakra and down and out through the bottom of your feet into the ground. This neutralizes the emotions and heightens your frequency.

6. Stare at the flame of a lit candle with as little blinking as possible. This relaxes the mind to release the ego state. It also helps in focus.

7. Stare into your eyes in a mirror, blinking as little as possible; allow the mirror to go black. This allows you to go into your subconscious mind to see beyond your reality.

8. Walk slowly and deliberately. This slows your nervous system down to relax you.

9. Visualize something as if it has already happened
   and feel it in your body. This is the ultimate
   technique for manifesting reality.

10. With or without a mala, repeat a mantra or
    affirmation multiple times, focusing only on what
    you are saying. This focuses the mind and manifests
    reality.

11. Color in a coloring book. This relaxes the mind to
    allow creativity to flow.

12. Dance without caring what you look like; feel your
    body move. This is a free-flowing expression from
    source.

13. Express your creativity in whatever ways you enjoy
    (drawing, painting, ceramics, jewelry making, etc.).
    This opens your mind to expansiveness.

Practices For Observing Spacecraft

The following methods are different ways you can enhance
your clairvoyance and observe spacecraft with your eyes
and mind. I have used all of these successfully to
experience craft.

Soften focus

On a clear or mostly clear night, go outside and sit
comfortably or lay down so you can see a good portion of
the sky. Relax your eyes to a very soft gaze, so your
peripheral view is activated. Allow your mind to drift into a
daydream-like state.

When you are in this alpha state, you may experience blinking light activity that isn't an airplane. You may also see orbs of energy glowing in different colors. The color indicates the amount of energy that is being generated by the craft or being. Red and orange are a lower amount of energy, whereas green and blue are much higher energy off-put.

You can also do this inside a house or building to experience seeing higher dimensional beings. You may see sparkles of light or distinct flashes out of the corner of your eye of various colors. Your eyes are not playing tricks on you. Your mind has the ability to see much more than what you think.

Blue grid

With the blue grid method, you can do this during the daytime or at night. Sitting or lying down comfortably, imagine a shimmering blue line grid overlayed on the sky. Hold the grid in your mind's eye. When you do this, you are actively removing the veil, creating a view into a higher dimension. Crafts that reside in higher dimensions become visible to you as you are in a higher state of frequency.

Remote viewing

You can experience craft and beings using remote viewing techniques. This one can take some practice. Get yourself into a meditative state. Once you are relaxed, your mind can travel to a specific location, allowing you to see with your mind's eye details of what is happening in a far-off location.

Method 1: For those of you who want to practice this, I recommend having a partner who can do it with you. Have the person decide on a specific day and time they will allow you to focus on them and what they are doing, what they are wearing, if they are with other people or alone, etc. Before starting, get into a meditative state. At the specified time, take about 15 minutes to really tune into them. Try to see as much detail as you can and take notes. Have your partner make notes on what they were doing and wearing at the specific time so they don't forget their own details. Do this multiple times over multiple days. Compare notes on what you saw and experienced versus what they were actually doing and wearing. The more you practice and acknowledge the things you did get right, the more you will trust and hone this ability.

Method 2: For those of you who want to practice this, I recommend having a partner who can do it with you. Have your partner draw a symbol with specific colors away from your location on a specific day and time that you can focus on. Before starting, get into a meditative state. At the specified time, take about 15 minutes to really tune into the symbol and the colors you see. Try to see as much detail as you can and take notes. Do this multiple times over a span of a couple of weeks. Compare your notes with the actual symbols drawn.

In the next chapter, we will explore different ways to communicate with extradimensional beings.

Chapter 15
Ways to Connect and Receive Guidance, Part 2

"So, while the body is asleep, the spirit is having many different adventures on its own. It can travel anywhere in the world, or go to the spirit side and converse with its guides and the masters and elders or to get more information, and attend classes and take training."
— Dolores Cannon, The Convoluted Universe, Book 2

The following methods are tools you can use to practice and enhance your communication with extradimensionals and other beings.

Dream State

Before you go to bed at night, take time to call in a visitation while you sleep. You could ask for specific healing. You can ask for something definitive which will let you know you were with other-dimensional beings. Be sure to journal your dream(s) when you wake up in the morning right away. Do this regularly and observe if there is a pattern of communication, including symbols or images you experience.

You may also practice astral traveling, which you may already do naturally without knowing it. Astral travel is the ability of a person's spirit to travel to distant places. This is one type of having an out-of-body experience. The physical body remains in bed, but the soul's essence travels wherever it chooses. Before going to bed, you can program your mind that you are going to travel to a specific location at a specific time during the night, perhaps to meet up with a person or group of people. Make a plan with a partner or a group of people who will participate in the experiment. In the morning, take note of anything you remember. Compare your notes with the others.

Automatic Writing

Get yourself in a meditative state to connect to your galactic beings. Be sure to raise your vibration and only allow in positive, light-focused beings. When you feel ready, you can start writing freely with pen and paper or typing on the computer. Just let the words flow without mentally thinking about it. Don't edit yourself. You may also choose to write out questions ahead of time. Once your mind is clear, let the answers just flow through you without judgment on the answers. You may be surprised at what comes through.

Telepathy

Higher-dimensional beings use telepathy as a way to communicate, rather than with verbal words. It allows more information to be disseminated in a short period of time. You can practice this technique with another person, with animals, and with plants. The more you practice, the better you get, and the more you trust yourself.

Method 1 – Sending and Receiving: There are numerous ways to practice telepathy with another person. I will describe a simple yet effective one in this section. Feel free to try other techniques as well. For this practice, sit in front of your partner with your knees touching. Stare into each other's eyes for about five minutes. Press your foreheads together, still staring into the eyes, for another minute. You really want to create a connection with them. Partner 1 will then imagine a symbol or a word (decide ahead of time if you wish to work with symbols or words for the exercise) in their head and energetically send it to Partner 2. Partner 2 will write down the symbol or word they are getting in their head. Partner 1 will send another symbol or word, repeating this up to 10 times. Then the partners will trade places so that Partner 2 is sending and Partner 1 is receiving.

Method 2 – Animal Communication: To do this, sit, breathe, and relax. Imagine the animal sitting across from you. Feel light within your heart. Sense, see, and feel the light within their heart. Purposely send light energy from your heart to their heart and let it flow back and forth. Allow light to expand into a bubble of light around you and the animal. Imagine giving them pets and love, rubbing their ears or belly. Tell them you love them so much. Thank them for letting them talk to you. See what energy the animal has at first. This can be a feeling in the body, words, or images. The biggest thing is trusting what you get. Write it down. Once you get the feeling, you can start asking questions. Ask the animal if there is anything they want to tell you. Let the answers flow.

You can also send images to the animal of what you would like them to know. For instance, with my dog Jaxx, I regularly sent him images to show him he was only supposed to go potty outside the house. He was a rescue dog, and when we got him, he had an issue with peeing inside. After some time of doing this, he stopped peeing in the house. I have also used this method with Jaxx and my cats to let them know I love them. I can observe they understand me by their actions when I do this, and I can feel their love back.

Method 3 – Plant Communication: This technique is similar to communicating with animals. Plants are energy beings and can send and receive information to other plants as well as to people. To do this, breathe and relax. Sit or stand next to the plant or tree. Feel light within your heart. Sense, see, and feel the light within their spirit. Purposely send light energy from your heart to their spirit and let it flow back and forth. Allow light to expand into a bubble of light around you and the plant. Tell them you love them so much. Thank them for letting them talk to you. See what energy the plant has at first. This can be a feeling in the body, words, or images. The biggest thing is trusting what you get. Write it down. Once you get the feeling, you can start asking questions, such as "is there anything you want to tell me?"

Of the three methods described, you will get the most accurate, real-time feedback from a human partner. All of these take practice, so don't get discouraged if it doesn't come naturally to you. It is important to be aware all living things have a spirit and can communicate. The more we appreciate their sentient nature, the more we can expand our communication with other-dimensional beings.

Communicating Through Regression

Regression is a form of deep relaxation, also known as hypnosis. You can do self-hypnosis, although some people find it's easier to trust the process if a skilled regression therapist leads the session. Once you are in a deep enough relaxation, imagine your spirit guides, angels, galactic family, deceased loved ones, or whoever you might want to call on being with you in a safe space. You can ask them questions or simply receive any guidance they may have for you in that moment. Allow the information to flow into you. When you come out of the relaxed state, write down what you saw and the messages you got.

Over my years as a regression therapist with numerous clients, this has been a powerful technique for communicating with other-dimensional beings. Those in a relaxed state are able to really see, feel, and hear their guides. The experience is as real as if it were happening in a completely awake state.

Vocal Channeling

The actual practice of vocal channeling is beyond the scope of this book, but I mention it because it allows direct communication to flow through you. The person who acts as the channel can be in a light trance where they are still aware of themselves being present, or they can be in a complete trance where they have no memory of what was

CONNECTION TO THE COSMOS

coming through them or anything in between. The entity that is being channeled will speak through the person from their own point of view.

Channeling requires your body to allow a lot of high vibration energy to move through it, so there are some things you can do to help prepare the body for this practice. Meditate regularly and practice raising your vibration to a higher state of frequency. Your mind is powerful in making this happen. Drink plenty of water to flush away toxins and other pollutants. Don't eat too much heavy protein. Move your body every day to release stuck energy. If channeling is something you have an interest in, there are great resources to help you do this. You can start by reading, *Opening to Channel: How to Connect With Your Guide* by Sanaya Roman and Duane Packer. There are teachers who teach courses on this as well.

When you decide you are ready to connect with higher dimensional beings, it is important you have worked through your shadows to clear out the monsters of your mind. Learn to face your fears and observe your reactions and emotions. When you initially encounter something unknown, your ego may try to protect you. Practice relaxing into the experience. There is nothing that can harm you because you are everything. You are in complete control of your life and your mind.

When you come from a place of curiosity rather than fear of the unknown, you will see things from a completely different perspective. The higher your vibration, the more potent you are in attracting higher dimensional beings to interact with. Know and trust your experiences as being real, even if there is no physical proof. Remember, the mind does not know the difference between when your eyes are open versus closed. The truth is inside you.

In the next chapter, I take you on a journey to experience your parallel non-Earth lives.

Chapter 16
Journey to Experience Your Parallel Non-Earth Lives

"She wasn't a constellation. She was a galaxy."
— Nitya Prakash

A s a past life regression therapist for the last several years, I have been able to guide my clients to experience other lives they have lived. A lot of the lives have been Earth-based, while other lives have been in other dimensions, realms, and locations not based on Earth.

One client experienced herself as a tree that lived for a thousand years. Another client observed herself as an entire planet that was destroyed by the fear-based beings living on it. Yet another client was an energy force of creativity that swept through the Earth. Other clients have explored extraterrestrial lives from other star systems. For some, this may be their first or only life on Earth. For others, they may have numerous Earth lives. Although I believe we all have had lives in different places and dimensions, not everyone is ready to experience those. The ego can be very protective.

In doing this work and understanding quantum mechanics, what I have come to know is there really is no past or future. All timelines exist simultaneously at the quantum level. So now, instead of talking about *past* lives, I prefer to use the term *parallel* lives. We have the ability to explore all of these different realities when we go deep enough into relaxation.

The following is a meditative journey to experience your parallel non-Earth lives. I highly recommend you record the meditation to play back to yourself. You may wish to do this journey multiple times to see if new lives reveal themselves to you or if you get deeper clarity about a particular life. You may wish to hire a professional Regression Therapist to help you explore these lives if you find it difficult to get deep enough to visualize.

Trust the images coming to you, even if you think you are making it all up. We cannot create realities in our heads we haven't already experienced at some level. Give yourself permission to take this journey. Get yourself into a comfortable position sitting or lying down.

Meditative Journey to Experience Your Parallel Non-Earth Lives

Go ahead and close your eyes and start taking some nice deep long breaths. Adjust your body so that you are comfortable and relaxed. Take a deep breath in and hold, then release, letting out all of the air. Take another deep breath in and hold. As you breathe out, your muscles relax. Tension is leaving the body. Continue to breathe, and as you do, your body becomes more and more relaxed. You are safe. All is well.

In your mind's eye, imagine a beautiful stream of white sparkling light above your head, like a waterfall. Open up the top of your head, your crown chakra, to let the shimmering white light flow into your head and make its way through your body, down behind your eyes, into your neck and shoulders, down into your arms, your chest, moving now through your hip area, into your legs and then out through your feet and into the ground. Continue imagining this stream of white light, like a waterfall, a river moving through you. As it moves through you, it relaxes every part of your body. It is removing any blocks or tension you may be holding on to. Allow it to move freely from the top of your head and down through your body and out of the bottom of your feet into the ground.

Each breath you take gets you deeper and deeper into your subconscious mind, more and more relaxed. The white shimmering light pours into the top of your head, cleansing away the debris, the cobwebs. Every sound takes you deeper and deeper. All is well. All is well. You are going to go on a journey to experience a parallel non-Earth life. Allow yourself to have this experience. You are connected with the universe. You are one with the universe. All of the memories and experiences are there for you to tap into, to remember who and what you are. You are more than this Earth body.

As you are relaxed, imagine every cell in your body vibrating. Notice how each of the cells is vibrating together with the other ones around it. All of your cells are in harmony with each other. As you are watching this vibration, the frequency begins to increase, and the vibration is getting faster. Your individual cells are starting to get fainter as the vibration increases. Your body is lighter as your vibration gets higher and higher. You are more and more relaxed.

In front of you, imagine a sparkling elevator of light. This elevator has the ability to take you to different lives you are currently living, both on Earth and elsewhere. It transcends time and space. All things, all memories, and all experiences are available through this elevator. See the elevator door shimmering gold. As the doors open, go ahead and step inside of the elevator and let the doors close behind you. As you do so, your cells begin to vibrate even faster. You can feel the tingling sensation throughout your body as the elevator begins to move. Trust that the elevator will take you to the life you desire to see at this time. It will take you to a life that is beyond Earth. Perhaps in a different dimension or a different location in space.

As the elevator is coming to a stop, you are ready to explore a new life, a new reality. The elevator has stopped, and the doors open. Now step out of the elevator and look down at the ground. Look at your feet. What do you see? What kind of ground are you seeing? What are you standing on? What do your feet look like? Are they bare, or do they have a covering of some sort? Pay attention to how your body feels. Do you get a sense of if you are male or female or androgynous? Are you wearing any clothes? What does your body look like, if you have one?

Look all around at the environment you have just stepped into. What do you see? Are you outside, or are you inside of a structure? Take in all of the details. Are there others there with you, or are you alone? If there are others, what do they look like? Are they the same or different from you? You have access to all of the information you need to know about this life, right here in this time and place. Allow the answers to come to you as I ask the following questions:

Where are you located in this life? Is it somewhere on Earth or in a different location? Are you in a different dimension, or are you in 3rd and 4th dimensional reality? What is your purpose in this life? Do you have a job? If so, what is it? Do you have a family? How do you spend your time in this place? There is a reason you are seeing this life right now. What do you need to know about this life? What wisdom have you gained in this life? How is this life connected to your current Earth life?

Take a few moments to explore this life and get an overview of the entire timeline. Let the visions and the feelings flow through you. You are safe.

In front of you once again is the elevator. Move over to the elevator. As the doors open, step back inside. The doors close, and once again, you can feel the energy inside of the elevator. It is raising your vibration, taking you to another time and place to observe a second life you are currently living. Taking you to a non-Earth life, trusting the elevator will stop at the perfect place for you to explore. As the elevator comes to a stop, the transition has happened. The doors open to a new time, a new place, a new reality. Step outside the elevator and look down at your feet. Look at the ground.

What do you see? What kind of ground are you standing on? What do your feet look like? Are they bare, or do they have a covering of some sort? Pay attention to how your body feels. Do you get a sense of if you are male or female or androgynous? Are you wearing any clothes? What does your body look like, if you have one?

Look all around at the environment you have just stepped into. What do you see? Are you outside, or are you inside of a structure? Take in all of the details. Are there others there with you, or are you alone? If there are others, what do they look like? Are they the same or different from you? You have access to all of the information you need to know about this life, right here in this time and place. Allow the answers to come to you as I ask the following questions:

Where are you located in this life? Is it somewhere on Earth or in a different location? Are you in a different dimension, or are you in 3ʳᵈ and 4ᵗʰ dimensional reality? What is your purpose in this life? Do you have a job? If so, what is it? Do you have a family? How do you spend your time in this place? There is a reason you are seeing this life right now. What do you need to know about this life? What wisdom have you gained in this life? How is this life connected to your current Earth life?

Take a few moments to explore this life and get an overview of the entire timeline. Let the visions and the feelings flow through you. You are safe.

Allow yourself to float away from that life towards the bright white light. You are now surrounded by pure source energy, feeling the love, feeling the unity. You have a deeper understanding you are more than just your one life on Earth. You are a multi-dimensional being that resides in multiple locations. You can access any of those timelines whenever you desire. All of this is inside of you.

Counting backward from five to one, you will begin to come back to the current time and place. Five, you are bringing back the full awareness of the two lives you just experienced. Four, you are more than your Earth life. You are multi-dimensional. Three, you are coming back, becoming aware of your consciousness, remembering the wisdom you gained in those lives. You remember what the connection is to your current Earth life. Two, you are coming back closer and closer, starting to wiggle your fingers and toes. One, you are back to your body. You can slowly open your eyes in your own time.

Remember who and what you are. You are love. You are one with the Universe. Thank you so much for taking the time to go on this beautiful journey with me.

JOURNAL EXERCISE:

Life 1

Describe in detail what you saw and how you felt in Life 1:

What was the wisdom you gained in Life 1?

What was the connection of Life 1 to this current Earth life?

Life 2

Describe in detail what you saw and how you felt in Life 2:

What was the wisdom you gained in Life 2?

What was the connection of Life 2 to this current Earth life?

What is the awareness you have now by observing these 2 lives?

Chapter 17
Bringing It Home to You

*"We are all connected! We are also individuals. We have
our own individual selves here on this earth, but there is a
part of us that is connected to everyone and everything
else. We are all ONE. Begin to move your awareness into
this understanding and look at everything
around you as if it is part of you."*
— Rachel D. Greenwell, How to Wear a Crown: A
Practical Guide to Knowing Your Worth

T hank you for taking this journey with me. Some of
you may feel a sense of relief, knowing you are not
alone. For those who have had experiences with
extradimensional beings, I hope you feel validated and
know you are not crazy. All of your experiences are real. If
you read this because you were simply curious, my wish is
you have a broader understanding of UFO and alien
phenomena and can discern the information out there
regarding this topic. Is the messaging fear-based or one of
love? I encourage you to choose the path of love.

You are so much more than this 3rd density Earth life. This
is a mere speck of dust in the vastness of all that you are.
Take time to embrace all of your parallel lives and realities.
When you raise your vibration, you have the opportunity to
experience the extraordinary, to go beyond whatever self-
imposed limitations you have. You are one with everyone
around you. You are one with your galactic family. You are

One with the Universe. There is no separation. The true nature of reality is LOVE.

Our galactic family is always here to guide us to a greater awakening within ourselves. When we connect with higher dimensional beings, we connect to our higher evolved selves. We remember where we came from. We experience the inclusion of all life forms without judgment. We understand the non-duality nature, which is truth. We let go of polarity and allow ourselves to experience the beauty of 4th density 5th dimension reality.

The tools and techniques I shared can be used to enhance all aspects of your life. You can enhance your intuition and trust the information you are receiving. You can connect to your galactic family and guides, as well as higher dimensional beings, including fairies, Ascended Masters, and angels. Everything is inside of you. You do not need external validation when you integrate and accept all of the wisdom inside you. Source energy is always there for you to tap into. You are a powerful creator of your reality. Awaken and embrace who and what you really are.

As you move forward in this life, let go of your judgments of yourself and others. Forgive yourself. Love yourself. When you come from a place of self-love, you have the capacity to extend love to others in the world. That's what we all need—love and understanding.

Don't dim your light to fit in. Shine your authentic light so your soul tribe can recognize you. Surround yourself with uplifting, supportive people. You are a magnet.

If you practice the techniques and allow yourself to come from a place of love and observe from a higher level of perspective, you will be prepared to welcome our Galactic brothers and sisters without fear if and when 3rd density First Contact happens. You will know you are one and the same. You can help share the message that we are all one. We are all connected. We all come from Source.

Final channeled message through Lisa from Arcturian Uluru:

"We are the Arcturians. We come to you with a final message that you are from the source of love. You are more energy than you are physical. You are powerful creators, and the more you play with raising your vibration, the more you will experience true joy and unity with all.

Do not be afraid of this work. It is for your own awakening. Trust your experiences and your wisdom. Give yourself more credit. You are extraordinary. You are everything and everyone. There is no separation.

We come in love. We wish to help humanity wake up, to let go of fear and judgment. We are here to remind you of who and what you are and where you come from. Expand your mind, your reality. Allow in new levels of understanding and integration.

Call on us when you need extra support for emotional healing. You are not alone. We love you."

Lisa and Arcturian Uluru

BIBLIOGRAPHY

Campobasso, Craig. *The Extraterrestrial Species Almanac: The Ultimate Guide to Greys, Reptilians, Hybrids, and Nordics*. Massachusetts: Red Wheel/Weiser, LLC. 2021.

Danaan, Elena. *A Gift From the Stars: Extraterrestrial Contacts and Guide of Alien Races*. 2020.

Fenton, Bruce and Daniella Fenton. *Exogenesis: Hybrid Humans: A Scientific History of Extraterrestrial Genetic Manipulation*. Massachusetts: New Page Books. 2020.

Horn, Arthur David and Lynette Anne Mallory-Horn. *Humanity's Extraterrestrial Origins: ET Influences on Humankind's Biological and Cultural Evolution*. Silberschnur. 1997.

Hynek, Dr. J. Allen. *The UFO Experience: a Scientific Inquiry*. Ballantine Books. 1972.

Johnston, Sunny Dawn. *Invoking the Archangels: a Nine-Step Process to Heal Your Body, Mind, and Soul*. Hierophant Publishing. 2012.

Lapseritis, Jack "Kewaunee." *The Psychic Sasquatch and Their UFO Connection*. Washington: Comanche Spirit Publishing. 1998.

Lapseritis, Kewaunee. *The Sasquatch People and Their Interdimensional Connection*. Washington: Comanche Spirit Publishing. 2011.

MacLaine, Shirley. *Out on a Limb*. New York: Bantam. 1983.

MacLaine, Shirley. *Dancing in the Light*. New York: Bantam. 1985.

Masters, Dr. Michael P. *Identified Flying Objects: A Multidisciplinary Scientific Approach to UFO Phenomenon*. Montana. 2019.

Roman, Sanaya and Duane Packer. *Opening to Channel: How to Connect With Your Guide*. California: HJ Cramer Inc. 1987.

Royal, Lyssa and Keith Priest. *Visitors From Within: Extraterrestrial Encounters and Species Evolution*. North Carolina: Granite Publishing, LLC. 1999.

BIBLIOGRAPHY

Royal-Holt, Lyssa and Keith Priest. *The Prism of Lyra: An Exploration of Human Galactic Heritage.* Arizona: Light Technology Publishing, LLC. 2011.

Salla, Michael E. *Exopolitics: Political Implications of the Extraterrestrial Presence.* Arizona: Dandelion Books. 2004.

Salla, Michael E. *Galactic Diplomacy: Getting to Yes With ET.* Hawaii: Exopolitics Institute. 2013.

Sitchin, Zecharia. *The 12th Planet.* Avon. 1976.

Strieber, Whitley. *Communion: A True Story.* Texas: Walker & Collier. 1988.

Thompson, Lisa. *Sacred Soul Spaces: Designing Your Personal Oasis.* Washington: Mystic Manta Publishing. 2018.

Thompson, Lisa. *Sacred Soul Love: Manifesting True Love and Happiness by Revealing and Healing Blockages and Limitations.* Washington: Mystic Manta Publishing. 2019.

von Däniken, Erich. *Chariots of the Gods? Was God an Astronaut.* Germany: Econ-Verlag. 1968.

ACKNOWLEDGMENTS

This book has been nearly 50 years in the making. I first want to thank my mother, Sharon Rosenberger, for her pioneering spirit in the early 1970s. She broke out of her childhood religious mold to forge a path into metaphysical science. Although I was angry when she moved us to Yelm, Washington, in 1986, I am grateful for all that I came to learn through the Ramtha School of Enlightenment. I appreciate her openness and encouragement as I have had my spiritual awakenings.

I am grateful for my loving and supportive husband, Skip Thompson. He trusted me enough to move our family to Hawaii at the end of 2020, which allowed me to fully step into my truth as a Galactic Ambassador. He's willingly along for the ride of a lifetime as we illuminate and educate about our galactic family through our UFO tours and my other teachings.

I am thankful for the support and guidance of my friend and mentor, Sunny Dawn Johnston. She has been there every week for the last three years to cheer me on and guide me in my business and personal life. She is the epitome of *Service to Others* and has been a huge inspiration for how I run my business.

I have gratitude for my friend and mentor, Linda Joy. She has helped me to get clear on my message and has been a great supporter of my business and personal life.

I want to thank my friends who have validated, supported, and encouraged me on this journey of galactic exploration, including Jennifer Hay, Irene Eno, Tammy Cantrell, Lee Michael Walczak, Tracie Mahan, Lisa Holm, Jodie Harvala, Kris Voelker, April DeMille, Brittany Farmer, Shanda Trofe, Desiree Watson, Arsha Fine, Kyra Schaefer, Brandi Strieter, Kris Groth, GG Rush, Kathy Small, Linda Hansen, Trina Johnson, Kate Shipp, Sharon Eistetter, Gina Black, Suzy Johnson, Ava Young, Devyn Pederson, and Alena Gourley.

And finally, I am forever grateful to my galactic family for always being there in the higher dimensions and making an appearance when asked.

ABOUT THE AUTHOR

Dr. Lisa Thompson is a Best-Selling Author, Speaker, Galactic Ambassador, and Intuitive Transformational Coach specializing in Human Design, Past Life Regression and Sound Healing. She supports and empowers women to intentionally design their best life by living from their *yes*, so they can embrace self-love, trust their intuition, and gracefully move forward through their fears to take inspired action to live a life they love.

Lisa is the best-selling author of *Sacred Soul Love: Manifesting True Love and Happiness by Revealing and Healing Blockages and Limitations* and *Sacred Soul Spaces: Designing Your Personal Oasis*. She has also contributed to four international best-selling compilation books, including *Life Reimagined*, *The Wild Women's Book of Shadows*, *Manifestations*, and *Inspirations*.

She is a frequent contributor for Aspire Magazine, a sought-after media guest and virtual event speaker and has shared the virtual stage with many leading visionaries, including Martha Beck, Neale Donald Walsch, Dr. Sue Morter, Gregg Braden, and Dr. Bruce Lipton.

Lisa earned a PhD in Organismal Biology and Anatomy from the University of Chicago and was a professor of Biology specializing in anatomy, physiology, and evolution of animals.

She has created eight oracle decks and designs intentional jewelry inspired by her passion for travel and nature. She loves teaching online classes and leads retreats in her home state of Hawaii. She leads night sky watch UFO tours under the company name of Big Island UFO Tours.

She is happily married to the love of her life, Skip, and lives on the Big Island of Hawaii with her three cats, Chana, Bindi, and Rajah, and dog, Jaxx. In her free time, she enjoys snorkeling, reading, traveling, and night sky watching.

For more information, visit www.DrLisaJThompson.com.

STAY CONNECTED WITH LISA

You can connect with Lisa online and via social media here:

Website:

www.DrLisaJThompson.com – sign up for her email list!

www.BigIslandUFOTours.com

Facebook:

www.facebook.com/DrLisaThompsonAuthor

www.facebook.com/BigIslandUFOTours

www.facebook.com/groups/sacredsoulspaces

www.facebook.com/groups/connectiontothecosmos

YouTube:

Connection to the Cosmos with Dr. Lisa Thompson

Connection to the Cosmos with Dr. Lisa Thompson explores "out of this world" topics with a wide range of fascinating guests. All things galactic, extra-dimensional, and other worldly will be up for conversation, storytelling and exploration.

Lisa regularly teaches online classes and leads destination retreats in Hawaii and abroad.

If you are visiting the Big Island of Hawaii, join her for Big Island UFO Tours to explore the night sky using advanced Gen 3 military night vision goggles.

Additional Services Lisa Offers:

Contactee Regression Session
Do you feel you have been contacted or temporarily detained by one or more alien civilizations, but you don't remember the details, or do you feel like you have made it up in your mind? You are not alone. It is more common than people think. Lisa is an Advanced Certified Past Life Regression Therapist who is trained to tap into your subconscious mind where all of your memories and experiences lie hidden. She can help you to reveal your memories in great detail so you understand the meaning of your experience and verify for yourself that it is, in fact, real. Sessions can be held in person and over Zoom.

Parallel Life Regression Session
Do you believe you have lived as a different alien species in a different world in a parallel incarnation? Lisa is an Advanced Certified Past Life Regression Therapist who is trained to tap into your subconscious mind where all of your memories and experiences lie hidden. She can help you to remember who you are in different times and locations. Sessions can be held in person and over Zoom.

170

Human Design Chart Reading

Learn who you were born to be in this Earth life with a personal Human Design chart reading. Human Design combines the modalities of Western Astrology, the I Ching, Hindu Chakra System, Kabbalah Tree of Life, Genetics, and Quantum Mechanics. Sessions are held over Zoom.

For more information, visit: www.DrLisaJThompson.com

Made in the USA
Middletown, DE
09 December 2022

16123490R00106